RECE

3 02

D0425822

MADRONA

The Art

OF THE

Wasted Day

Also by Patricia Hampl

PROSE

The Florist's Daughter

Blue Arabesque

I Could Tell You Stories

Virgin Time

Spillville
(with engravings by Steven Sorman)

A Romantic Education

POETRY

Resort and Other Poems

Woman before an Aquarium

AS EDITOR

The St. Paul Stories of F. Scott Fitzgerald

Burning Bright: An Anthology of Sacred Poetry
from Judaism, Christianity and Islam

Tell Me True: Memoir, History, and Writing a Life
co-edited with Elaine Tyler May

The Art

—— OF THE ——

Wasted Day

Patricia Hampl

VIKING

VIKING
An imprint of Penguin Random House LLC
375 Hudson Street
New York, New York 10014
penguin.com

Portions of this book first appeared in somewhat different form in
The Sophisticated Traveler (published by The New York Times), *Gulf Coast*,
Image, *The Iowa Review*, and *Not Less Than Everything* edited by
Catherine Wolff (HarperCollins, 2013).

"Lying in a Hammock at William Duffy's Farm at Pine Island, Minnesota"
from *Above the River: The Complete Poems and Selected Prose of James
Wright*. © 1990 by Anne Wright. Published by Wesleyan University Press.
Used by permission.

ISBN 9780525429647 (hardcover)
ISBN 9780698407497 (ebook)

Printed in the United States of America
1 3 5 7 9 10 8 6 4 2

Set in Fairfield LT Std
Designed by Cassandra Garruzzo

For Terrence

Prelude

Sometime around 1535, a good thirty years before the French Wars of Religion staked Catholic and Protestant heads on pikes around the Bordeaux countryside, in a gray stone castle deep in the wine country near Bergerac and Saint-Émilion, Pierre Montaigne, of a recently ennobled family, took the unprecedented step of hiring a lute player to awaken his child every morning. He was not an educated man, but he was an ardent father.

He followed a theory, probably picked up during his military years in Italy, his son later wrote, that "it troubles the tender brains of children to wake them in the morning with a start, and to snatch them suddenly and violently from their sleep, in which they are plunged much more deeply than we are." The lute followed Pierre Montaigne's boy, Michel, around the castle—"I was never without a man to do this for me."

Music—lyrical, wordless—was the sound track of his childhood, the ground beat of his existence. An inducement to reverie.

Though he reports that his nature was always "gentle and tractable," Michel Montaigne, celebrated in our time as "the first modern man" (and in English departments as the father of the personal essay, that most amateur literary form), confesses that he was in fact "so sluggish, lax, and drowsy" that he was a poor student when lessons required serious application. No one, he says, "could tear me from my sloth, not even to make me play."

He was otherwise engaged—floating on the charmed notes of that childhood lute, no doubt. Lolling in the lap of leisure, adrift on fey melodies handed down from the Provençal lays of the Troubadours.

There was fugitive genius in this indolence. "What I saw, I saw well," he says, cannily, much later, "and beneath this inert appearance nourished bold ideas and opinions beyond my years."

Montaigne found his vocation early, companioned by music plucked on sheep gut as he went up and down the staircase of his father's cold house, the same stony place where, years later, he would return from a life at court to sit alone in a room with words, to reveal his mind. Or really, to discover his mind.

He divined early the value of being sluggish, lax, drowsy . . .

He was not, as people now say, the first modern skeptic. He was the first modern daydreamer.

Contents

The Art

OF THE

Wasted Day

Timelessness

It begins—July afternoon—under the shade of the beechnut tree. The tree belongs to Mr. Kinney, the shade is ours. It must be 1953, because the Magnavox has just been delivered from McGowan's TV and Appliance on Grand. It's not just for watching Lucy, my mother says, already mistrusting it. "You're seeing history." She points to the first smudged image she allows us to see—the Koreans and Chinese and Americans signing their names in a big Bibley book. "Peace," she says, settling in with her cigs, the chipped cloisonné ashtray at hand.

An announcer drones from the glass box, murmuring names. One after another, men approach the heavy table to sign the book, each handing a fountain pen to the next. Mother taps her cig against the little Chinese ashtray, a gift, she tells me, from her uncle who was a U.S. Customs agent in San Francisco, half a world away from us in St. Paul. He got the ashtray when he broke an opium smuggling ring, she says proudly. He left the ashtray to her.

"Did he steal it?" I ask.

She looks startled. "Not exactly," she says uncertainly, turning back to the television. This is going to take a long time, the men handing the pen back and forth. History, it turns out, is boring.

So I come out here, throw myself on the ground where the feathers of the beechnut sway and tilt. The green filigree patterns the sky, light filters my face. It's hard (the ground), yet also soft (the sponge of lawn). I shut my eyes. The Customs agent uncle, dead before I was born, is standing on a San Francisco dock. Does he have a gun? He has a badge, that I see. He lifts the blue cloisonné ashtray out of a burlap bag, and a Chinese man has his hands up in the air. He has a long pigtail I recognize from the black-and-red lacquer tray Mother brings up with soup and saltines when we're sick in bed. There must be a gun somewhere, but where is it?

The scene fades, and a fresh image appears, our next-door neighbor Mr. Kinney, who presents himself in the dark for no reason. There he is, filling my mind.

Mr. Kinney is a widower. My mother says his wife has been dead "forever." A hush of respect hovers over this fact. Because he is a widower and because he "has money," he has a housekeeper. She doesn't like me. She wears a flowered apron trimmed with rickrack, and her designation—housekeeper—makes her slightly sinister. Who has a housekeeper? Not normal people. Only Mr. Kinney, a widower without children but with money. He owns the coke factory near the zoo, a place of foreboding, heaps of blackened coal, acrid, smoking. "They'll have to clean that up one day," my father says.

Mr. Kinney sits in his glassed-in sunporch before dinner, sipping whiskey from a lowball glass. He drinks after dinner too, slowly, meditatively. He reads, his old smooth head glowing under the floor lamp. He has decided against a television set, he informs my father who has inquired if, with the windows open in summer, the sound of the Magnavox carries. We've all noticed the nasty bark of the laugh track, nothing like real laughing.

He's decided to stick with books, Mr. Kinney tells my father. He also listens to the radio as Halsey Hall calls the ball game in a voice juicy from a chewed cigar. You can see Mr. Kinney leaning back in his sloping armchair, eyes closed, following the game. Another person who shuts his eyes to see. In the summer you can hear the metallic *chink* of ice in the lowball glass. *He drinks alone,* my mother says.

When you close your eyes, you see and hear things you didn't notice before, though they must have been there all along. It's not that you make things up—you *notice* things. Maybe that's a kind of making up? Hard to say. But it's all more real than history blatting away in the living room where my mother stares at the gray glass, tapping her cig against the little saucer of the blue ashtray taken from the Chinese man with his hands above his head. Mother is still there, as the pen passes from a Chinese man to an American and on to the next and the next. She's happy. She's watching peace occur in the wide world. Peace is vital to her: *We had to drop the bomb, darling. It ended the War. It saved lives.*

But now, *here,* under the shade of the beechnut, I float past the Customs agent and the Chinese smuggler, over the disapproving face of Mr. Kinney's housekeeper, above mild

Mr. Kinney himself, swirling his oily drink on his sunporch. Day after day, night after night during my endless girlhood I float away like this.

My father says Mr. Kinney takes his bourbon on the rocks. Mr. Kinney is slipping down a craggy cliffside under a shower of coal dust. He teeters off his sunporch—*takes his bourbon on the rocks, drinks alone.*

There's something orchestral about all this. My father's voice, my mother's, the *chink* of ice, the echo chamber of that word—*alone*. A melodic moan struggles out of the sad-souled vowel at the word's dead center—the sob at the core of *alone. O!* The stagey hand-on-heart intonation at the beginning of poems that Great-Aunt Aggie recites—*O to be in England, O for a beaker of the warm South . . . Bourbon on the rocks. Well, it's sad, darling—he drinks alone. O! O!*

Words are partly thoughts, but mostly they're music, deep down. Thinking itself is, perhaps, orchestral, the mind conducting the world. Conducting it, constructing it. I sense this instinctively.

There is no language for this, not then, not even now, this inner glide, articulation of the wordless, plotless truth of existence. Life is not made up of stories, much as I adore them— Charlotte, Heidi, Caddie Woodlawn. Really, life is—*this*. It's a float, my body a cloud drifting along, effortless but aware. Drifting over the world, seeing, passing along.

Years later, peering across from the Kinney sunporch to ours, Mr. Kinney's housekeeper glimpses me roiling around on the couch with my first boyfriend and reports this to my grandmother, who conveys the intelligence to my mother—

She had a hippie boy out there—with the vindicated face of a tattling teacher's pet.

At eight I don't yet see the hippie boys or the clasping and kissing, but already I recognize the look on the housekeeper's face. It is the aggrieved visage of the unloved, thwarted, and denied. The flaccid cheeks slip downward, the sour line of the lips tightens. That sharp eye on the prowl, passing from the back door to the trash can with her bag of refuse, frowning at me lolling under the shade of her employer's beechnut tree. She's a busybody.

She recognizes me too for what I am: her natural enemy. A girl up to no good, lazing my days away, conducting music no one else hears. A time-waster. A daydreamer.

Which poses a problem: in a few months we will make our First Confession. We have reached the age of reason. Sister says we now know the difference between Good and Evil. She has given us the buff-colored *Baltimore Catechism* and directed us to the "Examination of Conscience" at the back to help us prepare for our first whispered recitation in the basement of St. Luke's. The Ten Commandments are listed, each with its complement of sins and "occasions of sin," which are to be avoided.

I have located Disobedience (number 4) and Lying (number 8) as my province, as well as the diffuse "Unkind Gossip," an all-purpose sin that seems to belong to no particular commandment, but exists as an aura around all human relations. Then I reach the combined list of sins and occasions of sin for Commandments 9 and 10, where all the Coveting goes on. There, shockingly, without explanation, is the word. *Daydreaming.*

Busted. An official sin, ratified by the *Baltimore Catechism*. I stare at it, disbelieving.

To refuse to admit to a sin listed in the "Examination of Conscience" is a disobedience more profound—this I know—than the trivialities against my mother and father I've been toting up for presentation to Father Kennedy in the little curtained box in St. Luke's basement. A *bad confession* is the worst sin of all. Mortal.

But daydreaming, this effortless flight of the mind? I'm thunderstruck. Yet also oddly confirmed. A faint bell chimes within—of course the imagination is up to no good. You know that, you were born knowing that. It's the real, the true occasion of sin. Under the beechnut tree, leaves swishing, the sound of the oily sluice—*chink, chink-chink*—alone on the rocks. *O alone.* But connected to everything, conducting the unheard harmony that is the truest music. The sweetness of it, lolling under the filtered light of heaven. You possess everything that passes through the mind. It's divinity. That must be the sweetness.

That must be the sin.

I don't just mentally reject this sin. I tra-la my way past it. A higher editorial power takes over. I unsee it, unread it. That's part of this daydream paradise—unthinking my own thinking. I excise the word from the *Baltimore Catechism*, from my mind. I'm gripped by refusal. It's a form of loyalty. I'm never letting go of *this*.

The tendency to float, to depart, to *rest*—this power resides within me. It's right in there, jammed into the space where I've been taught conscience also resides—inside. *Lis-*

ten to your inner voice, children. It will guide you. Right here, Sister says, not reaching up to her wimpled head, but touching a pale hand to her obscure bosom under the gloomy tarp of her habit. Right *here.* That's where truth is. You always know—if you consult *here.* No one questions—I still have not questioned—that there is an inner voice to be heard.

I don't hesitate. I throw my lot with the occasion of sin. I already know (or believe—which comes to the same thing in my Catholic worldview) that daydreaming doesn't make things up. It *sees* things. Claims things, twirls them around, takes a good look. Possesses them. Embraces them. Makes something of them. Makes sense. Or music. How restful it is, how full of motion. My first paradox.

I couldn't care less what it's called. It's pure pleasure. Infinite delight. For this a person goes to hell.

Okay then.

Though I don't yet know it, though Sister has her hand on her breast, this is what is called *the life of the mind*. It's what I want to do. It's where I want to be. Right here.

F ast forward. More than forty years, and what's become of "the life of the mind"? Hand on heart, the inner voice still murmuring? I've taken my place, middle seat, my husband on the aisle, a plump woman already seated by the window. I fasten my seat belt, low and tight as instructed. My husband takes my right hand, gives it a squeeze, opens his book.

The plane taxis forward, the woman next to me is looking with pleasant curiosity out the window. Blue skies, no wind.

We lift off, levitating at a rather sharp angle, without shimmy or rattle or bobble. A confident plane. We're up cleanly at a sheer slant. And I'm dying.

It is impossible to breathe in this canister hurling itself on high. The thing is not properly pressurized. No one can breathe in here. We will all die, or—another possibility occurs in the same instant—we may land safely, but we'll be a planeful of brain-damaged droolers. Alive, but gone, gone.

I have picked up on the truth sooner than the others. But didn't teachers often say I was quick? In a moment these poor souls will be leaping from their places, madly clawing for air. At least I will die with dignity. My eyes fasten on a hopelessly unaware man farther forward on the aisle, sitting calmly with his newspaper open. I wait for him to leap up, hurl the paper aside, clutch his throat. He won't be dying with dignity. But I will. I sit still, frozen in my dignity.

The woman by the window has taken my left hand. She's stroking it. "You're all right," she's saying. "I'm a labor and delivery room nurse, and you're all right." Does she think I'm pregnant? I'm over fifty.

"You're all right," she keeps saying. Very annoying singsong. "Look at your hand."

I look. There it is. And her hand, stroking mine.

"See? It isn't blue. If you were dying your hand would be blue." It would? I realize I'm gasping. Loudly, raggedly.

I haven't been dying with dignity. I have been making—am still making—weird gagging sounds, desperate, wild. My husband looks alarmed. He has taken my other hand. I feel bound, and rip my hands away from these deluded handholders who somehow are managing to breathe in this airless cylinder.

The labor and delivery nurse hands me the airsickness bag from the seat pocket. "Breathe into this," she says, commanding now, not gentle. "Put the bag to your mouth, bend your head. Breathe. In. Out. Breathe. Out. Out. Deep *out*."

This I do. "You're having a panic attack," she says. "You aren't dying."

What does she know? Everything in me tells me I'm dying. I'm a writer. I trust my instincts, I live by my wits. But I do as she says, breathing deep into the bag. No one is leaping around. That gets through to me. Only my husband looks bug-eyed, leaning toward me, but no longer touching me because I have batted him away.

"You're not dying," the nurse repeats with irritating certainty. "You've got too much oxygen in your system. Breathe out. Deep. Deep! *Out!* We'll get that carbon dioxide level up. You're having a panic attack," she says again. She pats my leg briskly, not unkindly. She's seen this before.

She hits the call button. I'm given a glass of water. "Drink." Breathe, drink, live to see another day. Live to tell the tale.

"Better?" the nurse says pleasantly after the water is gone. A pat on the leg. "Better?"

Not really. Not dying, but not better. My husband is thanking her profusely. He's holding my hand. I allow this, my cold meat patty in his beautiful warm, dry hand. His beautiful hand I've always loved. I love it again, which is a sign I'm not dying. The nurse has turned back to the window, enjoying the bed of pillowy clouds we rest upon.

That was ten years ago. It took almost two weeks before I could breathe unconsciously again. For days I took deep greedy intakes of air, full of gratitude, but not entirely persuaded. Some inner monitor kept checking—yes, breathing, still breathing. I had struggled mightily with a fierce angel. A muscular dark devil. True, he had won, but I had been spared, left heaving on the roadside where we had contended, left to resume my fate.

A panic attack? But there had been no panic, not even a tingle of apprehension. I went from life to death—not what I "thought" or imagined was death, but the absolute sensation of extinction—without a signal, as if I'd been hit from behind by a Mack truck as I walked down a perfectly ordinary street. Mugged by death.

How I slept those weeks afterward. A slumberous swoon in the afternoon (I who was never a napper), and all night long, dreamless, content. I felt profoundly convalescent. It was heavenly. I yawned a lot, huge, openmouthed yawns. I couldn't yawn enough. I was tireless in my yawning.

I had not rested like this since . . . out of the deep folds of childhood, the beechnut tree wagged its scissored leaves above me, and faded away again.

Nor was this the only time I suffered a panic attack. The others (three) occurred on terra firma, not presenting themselves as death but as brainlessness.

Each time I thought I'd had a stroke. Again, no emotion, no awareness of "stress" or worry. Just suddenly, a closing down of the lower functions—or are they the higher functions? Specifically, I realized I didn't know what year it was. I was out of time, out of mind. Time itself was gone, had no meaning. Other scraps of basic info were missing, and a light mantle of oddity rested upon me, a rustling tissue of thin taffeta in place of what usually passed for my mind. I lost names, other dates, including my birthday (I clawed my way to that after a few moments), but it was the *oddity* that claimed me and defined the experience. Timelessness, airiness, self as a thinning, drifting cirrus cloud.

That's the best I can do—to call it oddity. Like a mystic who cannot describe transfiguration, I'm unable to capture this sensation of the loss of my mind—if that's what I had lost. I wasn't seizing the moment—the moment had seized me.

Of course I went to the ER. Tests, MRI, the questions (I did know who the president was and was proud of it, but I still didn't know the year). A pill was administered. *It will calm you*. I didn't feel uncalm. I felt . . . odd. Do you have an oddity pill?

Aside from sensing I really ought to know the year, it was not unpleasant. In fact, it was lovely as long as I didn't care about knowing the year and various other pieces of basic intel usually packed into the kit bag of my busybee mind.

The ER doctor came into my cubicle after the tests and labs.

"You've had a panic attack."

Oh, that.

"You're fine."

I threw into the wastebasket the prescription he gave me. The very idea of pills made me anxious, the only "stress" I experienced from my dive into the deep lake of oddity.

And again I slept. And slept. And was restored to myself in due course, trailing the tatters of some lost ease, that filmy taffeta oddity, the consolation prize, apparently, of being rattled out of myself, a blip on the flashing screen of adulthood. I'd "come back" from that other life, the one under the beechnut where my mind first appeared to me as a drifting cloud.

After all these years, still a Daydream Believer—that Monkees' bubblegum song of my girlhood. Still crazy after all these responsible years. Still looking for bliss in nothing at all, the cloudy mind moving over existence, outside time.

And then returned to what I thought of as my life.

And what is that—"my life"? Fifty years—more—and "the life of the mind," lolling under the beechnut, has long since morphed into a scrum of tasks jittering down the day.

Life conceived—and lived—as a to-do list. This is the problem. I sense I'm not alone. Fretful, earnest, ambitious strivers—we take no comfort in existence unfurling easefully *as God intended* (my mother speaking, a middling midwesterner who knew how to let things unfold without rush, her head wreathed with vagueness, the smoke of her cig circling upward).

For the worker bee, life is given over to the grim satisfaction of striking a firm line through a task accomplished. On to the next, and the next. Check, check. Done and done. It explains—and solves—nothing to call this workaholism.

Whatever happened to that Roman concept, first encountered in Intermediate Latin—*otium cum dignitate,* honorable leisure? The peace that passeth understanding that the classical world held as its ideal, the ease I'd touched under the beechnut tree, not knowing it would disappear, fade, elude me when the time came to stop throwing myself on the grass and looking up at the passing clouds. Never mind the necessity of a slave class to keep the *otium* basking on the secluded hillside villa portico under its shaded grape arbor. Still, where is the ideal at least, if not the way of life?

And what about Montaigne in his tower, retiring from public life to muse about how to die—or was it how to live? Whichever. Put that on the list: *Read Montaigne*.

So many books I keep meaning to read. I move the titles from one to-do list to another. I don't bother listing Proust anymore. I've read the opening pages about the madeleine cookie soaked in linden flower tea so many times, I've come to think of *In Search of Lost Time* as a short lyric. I get the picture, if not the story. I have time for vignettes, but not for narrative arcs. I start a novel, but keep breaking off to check my iPhone. I-Phone indeed—the busyness of me myself and I.

I've already read enough Montaigne (I've even taught him—The Art of the Personal Essay, Eng 5610) to know I'd like to waste my life the way he did, taking up one conundrum after another, plucked out of idiosyncratic curiosity, how he wrote his way around a subject for a while, dropped it, picked up another—*On Cannibals, On Experience,* on this, on that.

He called them essays, but he didn't mean a freshman theme. He used the word to show he wasn't a professional literary man, that he was just tossing off unbidden thoughts for his own interest. Accidentally, he invented a literary genre. The one I practice.

Yet, even before the essays, before my "work," I keep composing to-do lists. My most recent:

Return overdue books
Mammo appt
Mustard, garlic, milk (skim), bananas
Date of Thanksgiving this year?
Letters of rec: Greg, Jeff, Susan . . . who else???
Blurbs (3—actually read the books to the end)
Flowers to GK (mother's death—or was it father . . .
    ask Ellen)
Ants in kitchen. Traps? Poison? Hardware store?
Fish oil (helps against aging—Sue)
Overcoats to Goodwill
Czech phrase book for G (leaves Monday)
Memoir ms. from Montreal paralytic (bottom right
    pile)—READ/RESPOND
Furnace inspection (ticking sound)
Rose wilt (ask Joan? Judith?)
Check to Refugee Sanctuary (how much?)
Geraniums and sprengeri fern for the graves
Deadline
Dentist
Dish soap
Dog food

This organization (or attempt at organization) is meant to sweep away all the dumb tasks of the day so that Real Life can be lived. Real Life? What comes after dog food?

Onward to the night, which is to say insomnia, cell phone

on the bedside table, the mind drilling away with yet more frantic interior list-making. *Don't forget! Remember to . . . Have you . . . Did you . . . ?*

Whole decades can go this way—and have—not just in domestic detail, but awash in the brackish flotsam of endeavor, failure and success, responsibility and reward. My work, as I say with foolish vanity. Deadlines piled upon deadlines. That devilishly apt word *deadline,* the heart seizing as if shot, hands wringing for a reprieve—a week, a day? But delivering. Always delivering. You can count on me. That, in fact, is the problem. I never learned to follow Nancy Reagan's one piece of good advice: Just Say No.

Even with the arch refusal to friend anybody or to tweet abstemiously in 140 characters from the baroque song sheet of my jammed mind, even so, the daydream life, that prairie of possibility cherished from childhood, and beyond that into my delicious time-wasting youth—all that has been junked up with . . . with what? Reality? Life as it really is and must be for an adult?

Wasn't it Fitzgerald, St. Paul boy, first literary hero, who said bitterly toward the end of his life that "the natural state of the sentient adult is a qualified unhappiness"? By turns rhapsodic and vexed, he was more profoundly American in his ambition and his romance for the country—those *boats against the current, the dark fields of the republic rolling on under the night*—than he-man Hemingway with his fishing and hunting, his safaris and wars.

Eventually, Fitzgerald was fed up with striving, with what he called "the bitch goddess of success." In the depths of the

Depression (his own and America's) he wrote his "Crack-Up" essays when he couldn't bear the effort anymore—"my limitless capacity for toil." Another deadline-beset soul.

Another lifelong list-maker. He made his tragic hero into one too, the notebook found after poor George Wilson has shot Gatsby in his pool. The boyhood ambition outlined in his rigorous to-do list proves that Jimmy Gatz, a.k.a. Jay Gatsby, is the ultimate tragic American hero not because he was ruinously ambitious and something of a crook, but because he was an ardent self-improver:

> Rise from bed . . . . 6 a.m.
> Dumbbell exercise and wall-scaling 6:15–6:30
> Study electricity etc. .7:15–8:15
> Work . . . . .8:30–4:40 p.m.
> Baseball and sports 4:30–5:00
> Practice elocution, poise and how to attain it 5:00–6:00
> Study needed inventions 7:00–8:00
> General Resolves: No wasting time at Shafters . . . No more smoking or chewing Bath every other day Read one improving book or magazine per week Save $5.00 [crossed out] $3.00 per week Be better to parents

Jimmy Gatz followed a long lineage from that original American list-maker, Ben Franklin, whose *Autobiography* lays out the day like a time card to be punched, his list of improvements and self-creating instructions a handmade noose he fitted around his own neck, dragging his life forward, always forward. Or upward.

This list-making of a self-improving sort is an American

heritage from Franklin to Fitzgerald to us, the urgent organization of the day in the service of bettering oneself. Nothing
like the cloudy drifting under the beechnut that still beckons
(or haunts) after all these years. Up in the air, flying, higher,
higher, dying into a panic attack. Up, up (Fitzgerald's first
word, I read somewhere, was *Up*, inscribed by his mother in
his baby book), the American urgency for uplift. Or that four-
bit word—transcendence.

Reprimand to self: you dare to complain about a life rich in
tasks and duties and pleasures—rich with meaning? Daily
life, work you chose and profess to love, domestic detail, the
call and reply of other people's lives, the beloveds mixed in
there with everybody else who has a claim on you, the sheer
wants and requests, always heard as demands, the gnats of
need buzzing. Deadlines. Delivering. Always.

Not to mention the weights of the past, hanging like bells
gonging from your wrists. Memory is a tough boss, a micro-
manager sending too many memos. Even the realization, still
coming as a surprise: the shock of how happy you were in
love, for years, how long you were given to have and to hold.
Even though he's gone now, the bell of memory. The beautiful hand holding yours. Dust now.

We'll get to that.

And the flip side of memory, the sharp tableaux of error or
unkindness, embarrassment, missed chances—the troubles I
doled out surprisingly more unbearable than the wounds absorbed from others. The grinding gears of the private news-

reel, flickering anxiously in the dark night when a person should be unconscious, dreaming, not thinking. The scars of old heartbreaks that seared you, gave you a depth charge. Even they have value, a "fortunate fall" as every English major learns in the required Milton course.

And the main event—work, the years of writing, reading, editing, teaching, the focus on projects, book after book, assignment after assignment, the fact of having done, more or less, what you set out to do. Clawing your way from project to project, not thinking of it as clawing. Thinking of it as "my work." You sought the deadlines—they weren't coerced. You who come from people who were servants to "the rich," that aggrieved Fitzgerald term. The first generation in your line to go to college. Allowed to rise and shine.

You're complaining? It's called a full life. A good life. A lucky life. The friends it has brought, wild humor, some bright lights, charms and delights, long nights, early mornings, invitations, travel. Lucky you, as I keep saying.

Still, the sense of life being littered rather than lived.

Nor am I alone in this nostalgia for the lost nothing-moment that turns out to be—well, everything. The crucible of consciousness. The lovely wasteful vagary of the mind. Virginia Woolf tried to capture it:

If life has a base that it stands upon, if it is a bowl that one fills and fills and fills—then my bowl without a doubt stands upon this memory. It is of lying half asleep, half awake, in bed in the nursery at St Ives. It is of hearing the waves breaking, one, two, one, two, and sending

a splash of water over the beach; and then breaking,
one, two, one, two, behind a yellow blind. It is of hear-
ing the blind draw its little acorn across the floor as the
wind blew the blind out. It is of lying and hearing this
splash and seeing this light, and feeling, it is almost im-
possible that I should be here; of feeling the purest ec-
stasy I can conceive.

Even she gives up: "I could spend hours trying to write that as it should be written, in order to give the feeling which is even at this moment very strong in me. But I should fail (unless I had some wonderful luck)."

She is describing something so essentially offhand, so without narrative value, that nothing can be made of it. A gold so frail that it cannot be annealed into anything. It's gold, all right, but such an airborne mote of gold, it can never be fashioned. Still, it glimmers, haunts, beckons.

It's taken for dross. Waste. Yet in the end (and at the beginning—childhood) this glimmery bit is the only thing of value we possess. Its weight cannot be measured. It can never be lost or traded away. It's just . . . there. Or here—within. Sister touches her hidden breast—*It's right here, boys and girls. If you listen.*

It's the beam of consciousness glinting on experience, claiming it. That's why we all know what *Rosebud, Rosebud* means, whispered at the end of the movie—it's the fragment of self imprinted as the emblem of consciousness. What's left of the nugget of self, innocent yet apprehending reality. The embrace of the whole wide world of living.

Life, if you're lucky, is divided into thirds, my father used to say: youth, middle age, and "you look *good*." The dawn of that third stage winks, is just cutting me in the eye as I lift my hand against its rise. It isn't simply that at this point more life is behind me—behind any middle-aged person—than lies ahead. Middle-aged? Who am I kidding. An interviewer asked Alice Munro when she turned sixty how she felt to be middle-aged. *Middle-aged?* she said. *Who do you know who's 120?*

So it's not just about aging. But by the time you've worked long enough, hard enough, Real Life (which insists on being capitalized as if it were a personage with a proper name and a right to barge into this rental unit called your life) begins to reveal itself as something other than effort, other than accomplishment. Real Life wishes to be left to its own purposeless devices.

This isn't sloth, it isn't laziness. It isn't even exhaustion. It is a late-arriving awareness of consciousness existing for its own purpose, rippling with contentment and curiosity. One's own idiosyncrasy reveals itself as a pleasure, without other value—but golden, amusing, integrity hard-won and now at its leisure. Hand on heart, this life of the mind, lolling—tending to life's real business.

This latter stage of existence suggests that the ultimate task, the real to-do, is: waste your life in order to find it. Who said that? Or said something like that. Jesus? Buddha? Bob Dylan? Somebody who knew what's what.

Even the search for timelessness happens in history: mine is the first year of the notorious American Baby Boom. *You're a Boomer*—as if this generation were named for the bomb, the midcentury annihilator that was birthed about the time I was conceived. My mother murmurs again from her whirlwind of cigarette smoke: *We had to drop the bomb, darling. It ended the War. It saved lives.*

We got all the good stuff. The postwar hope-and-determination of our Depression-era parents was piled upon us, and we've been burning it up, the fossil fuel of earlier generations we spent without a care. No college debt, the "liberal arts" a reasonable study for four years, or six or eight. We had a preposterously long sense of our own youthfulness. And a limitless sense of our choices. Indulgences galore. Many certainties (Make Love, Not War! The Personal Is Political!), which we called rights and ideals. Never was a petulance as gleeful and buoyant as ours. We were even right about some of it. As if being right were the same as being real.

But now the Boomers are approaching the other side. Not death necessarily (though the time has begun when no one will say we were cut down too early). Not death, but we're reaching the other side of striving, past ambition. Good luck over there in pastureland.

What a surprise—to discover it's all about leisure, apparently, this fugitive Real Life, abandoned all those years to the "limitless capacity for toil." *What a hard worker you are:* always taken as a compliment. You can count on me. Smiling. Deadline met. Always.

You should try meditating or maybe yoga, yoga's good, someone suggested when I mentioned the fevered to-do lists, the sometimes alarming blood pressure readings, the dark-night-of-the-soul insomnia.

But meditating is just another *thing.* Yoga? Another task, yet another item for the to-do list. I find I cannot add another item. I'm done.

This particular battle between striving and serenity may be distinctly American. The struggle between toil and Real Life is a legacy we cannot reject or deny, coming to us as a birthright, the way a Frenchman expects to have decent wine at a reasonable price, and the whole month of August on vacation.

Maybe it goes all the way back to the Declaration of Independence, our "founding document." *Life, liberty, and the pursuit of happiness.* How proud I've always been, through the years of war protesting, the radical this and progressive that, to think of those words. What luck to be born into this buoyant heritage. What country was ever founded on the idea of happiness? Crazy. Good crazy. We aren't ideologues with a Five-Year Plan for civic betterment. We address happiness individually, conceive of it as an intensely personal project, each of us busy about our own bliss. Loved that, love it still.

But a canker forms on the rose. That unlikely word *happiness* charmed me, made me proud to be an American, not just for my own sake, but because everyone was enjoined to think about a personal project of delight—even if it couldn't be accomplished. Of course happiness is an illusion. Still, a beautiful one—I'll pledge allegiance to it.

But *happiness* is the only word in the Declaration of Independence triad that doesn't stand alone. Happiness is not, like life and liberty, a given, what Henry James called a donnée, the starter that gets you going on the story you write. Happiness in the American credo is a job. It must be *pursued*. It may not be clear what it *is*, but you better get hold of it. Your fault, sucker, if you can't somehow nab it for yourself.

I was mistaken. The essential American word isn't *happiness*. It's *pursuit*.

This is where the struggle is engaged—happiness as a project, a national enterprise. It is the root of Ben Franklin's list-making legacy, the burden of proof laid on the frail individual. Not happiness but its pursuit is the loneliness coiled in the heart of the American dream. That least dreamy of dreams, suited up with effort and determination.

Even a postmodern to-do list is not the answer. Go ahead—meditate, do yoga, buy probiotic foods, all that.

How about just giving up? Giving up the habit of struggle. Maybe it's a matter of giving over. To what? Perhaps what an earlier age called "the life of the mind," that phrase I fastened on to describe the sovereign self at ease, at home in the world when I decided to embrace that key occasion of sin—the daydream. Happiness redefined as looking out the window and taking things in—not pursuing them. Taking in whatever is out there, seeing how it beckons. And letting it go. On and on, out of range, a cloud passing, changing shape but still a cloud, still moving.

Other cultures labor, but what other nation enjoins each separate citizen to tackle happiness as a solo endeavor, a mission, this crazy paradox of a hunt for something that cannot, after all, be earned, but can only be bestowed from the mysterious recesses of life? Give it up. Waste the day, building up solidarity. Empathy is bred of aimlessness, just gazing, of having no agenda, and in a sense no self. The no self is the real self. Something like that.

That's what that model lounger Walt Whitman did, the un–Ben Franklin American. *I loaf and invite my soul. I lean and loaf at my ease, observing a spear of summer grass.* In this way he came to his great conception of national citizenship for Americans—*the dear love of comrades.*

It's no coincidence that our most American poet hands out this contrary notion—to loaf—in the midst of what he called in his westward-ho century America's "Democratic Vistas." Not much said about American vistas these days. Instead, plans for a wall on our southern border. And individualism? Does it lead to individual happiness or is its tragic destiny autocracy when it is claimed by a strongman?

The next generation, we're told, will not have the upwardly mobile lives we have had (or thought we were having). For starters, just look at their college debt. Ask the server in the hip farm-to-table restaurant who is reciting the evening specials from memory what the subject of his dissertation is, the PhD he finished four years ago.

Loafing and inviting your soul is not a prudent business plan, not a life plan, not even a recognizably American project Ben Franklin or Jimmy Gatz would care to . . . pursue.

But it begins to look a little like happiness, the kind that comes to claim you, unbidden. Stay put and let the world show up? Or get out there and be a flaneur, wandering along? Which is it? I'm looking out the window, I'm reading Whitman, I'm reading Montaigne. Also, I'm taking the dog for a long walk. She's nosing our way forward.

———————————

You do not need to leave your room. Remain sitting
at your table and listen. Do not even listen, simply
wait, be quiet, still and solitary. The world will freely
offer itself to you to be unmasked, it has no choice, it
will roll in ecstasy at your feet.
　　　　　—Franz Kafka, *The Blue Octavo Notebooks*

S ometimes the translation of that last line is rendered "the
world . . . will writhe in ecstasy at your feet." Hotter, definitely. Writhing is animal, sweaty, the world as struggling
beast or as lover in the heat of pain and pleasure. Rolling, on
the other hand, is slack, the sea of life whooshing and wash-
ing, lapping forward effortlessly.

The passage is most often translated as *roll*. I'm going with
writhe. I would rather believe that life rolls along, but everything points to the likelihood that it writhes.

There are many injunctions to solitude like Kafka's, all
easily googled, often copied into notebooks by the young and
ardent seeking direction, seeking wisdom, as I have copied
such lines in notebook and journal year after year from youth
to where I find myself now: the final third (if life is that neatly
sectioned, if I stay lucky that long). A rainy day and I've been
reading old notebooks, copying passages from my thickened
collection going back years, decades:

We seek retreats for ourselves, houses in the country, sea-shores, mountains. But . . . we have in our power to re-tire into ourselves. For there is no retreat that is quieter and freer from trouble than our soul . . . perfect tranquil-ity, the right ordering of mind.

—*Marcus Aurelius,* Meditations

A man [sic!—the sic added smugly in 1972, a robustly feminist period in my notebook life] can be himself only so long as he is alone; and if he does not love solitude, he will not love freedom; for it is only when he is alone that he is really free.

—*Arthur Schopenhauer,* Counsels and Maxims

Alone, even doing nothing, you do not waste your time. You do, almost always, in company. No encounter with yourself can be altogether sterile: Something necessarily emerges, even if only the hope of some day meeting your-self again.

—*E. M. Cioran,* Strangled Thoughts *[entire passage crossed out when Cioran's professed "Hitlerist" past came to light. "Never trust anyone that gloomy," written in damp, spreading ballpoint in the margin of the X'ed-out passage]*

*Without going out the door, you can know the
  whole universe.
Without looking through the window, you can see
  the ways of heaven.
The farther you go, the less you know.
Thus the sage knows without traveling,
sees without looking,
acts without doing.*

—*Lao-tzu,* Tao Te Ching

Most famously, Pascal's declaration that has dogged me longest: *All of humanity's problems stem from man's [sic! sic!] inability to sit quietly in a room alone.*

I first read that baleful line, living at home during college, itching to Get Out, the stereotypic midwestern frustration (though I didn't know I was a type—how original I thought my angst was). Lemme outta here. I thought the world (which I called inwardly "the great world") was not the problem (home was the problem). The world (a.k.a. freedom) was the solution.

These sour discouragements against setting forth, getting into the fray or the circus or whatever is out there, have sounded wise to me at one time or another, against my wanderlust will. Perhaps that was inevitable: I was taught ("trained," as they said) by cloistered nuns, paradoxically the first independent women I knew, and still the most vivid in memory (the only place they live anymore—Regina, Peronne, Immaculata, Mary Gertrude, Maria Coeli—all gone to glory, and none to take their places).

We caught a glimpse of their mysterious lives behind the filmy black curtain dividing the cloister from our side of the chapel. Enclosure, silence, chanted Latin murmurings. It was romantic and dead serious. They were staying in their rooms (cells!), watching the world make all its mistakes, praying and forgiving, waiting for the next madness so they could pray and forgive some more. There was the sense that precisely because they weren't out there they saw it all. Observation was not an act of experience, but of the imagination. This made perfect sense.

From the limitation of their enclosure, absurdly, they saw everything. Even their lack of experience was impressive, a badge of higher knowledge. *Sister,* a girl asked on a fine May morning, *can we have class outside in the courtyard, will you give us the green light?* The ancient nun, a tiny leprechaun (she hailed from Boston and wanted us in Minnesota to pronounce *been* as *bean*), looked mystified, but corrected the girl's grammar first: *May you—may you have class outside.* Then to the question itself: *What do you mean, dear, a green light?* she asked mildly. She'd been in the cloister over fifty years, and had never seen a traffic light. We were not disdainful. We were impressed, as if prehistory stood before us, alive and breathing.

They wore habits designed in the sixteenth century by their foundress, before the invention of buttons or hooks (buttons were *invented*?). They were forever replacing a straight pin to anchor a wimple or a veil. It was a graceful gesture, the hands light and deft fluttering around the fabric, white linen, black serge. The folds of the gowns were heavy, cut with couture severity, often patched tidily. They stayed in place—habits, veils, long lives in their minimalist cells.

The idea was to stay put, keep your lip buttoned while the secret door or window of the heart/mind opened of its own volition to reality. Stay. Don't seek. Let it all come at you, rolling or writhing.

And yet. Our most ancient metaphor says *life is a journey.* Not to mention the flyover midwestern heart, beating to Get Out. Midwesterners give over to the fiction of flight passionately, the desire to be Elsewhere is the native trait. Flyover, fly away.

We must set out, often without a destination, with only the instinct to search as a direction. Literature and religion are predicated on the notion of journey, movement—pilgrimage it's called in religion, plot in literature. Life's deepest pursuit is understood as a trudge: Moses on the forty-year desert camping trip, even Jesus isn't just nailed to the Cross. He treks the Way of the Cross to achieve Golgotha. The hajj to Mecca. And the Buddha? He doesn't *start* by sitting—first he roams.

Life is a journey. A hopeless cliché. But not its fault. Cliché is the fate of every fully absorbed truth. The stars, for example, do look like diamonds. You just can't say so.

Even storytelling, our simplest way to escape, begins with a journey—Dante in exile roaming with Virgil. And English literature (my major in college, still my major, it seems) starts with *The Canterbury Tales* ambling along the first English narrative pathway. The journey is plotless, mimicking life with its refusal to organize itself into a coherent "narrative arc." *The Canterbury Tales* is a series of stories, tall tales, beads strung on the thread of regional pilgrimage. Our literature begins as group tourism.

"Real" people—the randy Wife of Bath, the impoverished Knight—fabricate their fictions to amuse each other on their supposedly nonfiction way from south London to coastal Kent to venerate a saint. And of course to get away, just to escape. The pilgrimage is as much away as toward:

> *Whan that aprill with his shoures soote*
> *The droghte of march hath perced to the roote,*
> *And bathed every veyne in swich licour*
> *Of which vertu engendred is the flour . . .*
> *Thanne longen folk to goon on pilgrimages,*
> *And palmeres for to seken straunge strondes*

Springtime, after a winter cooped up, and everyone wants to hit the road. Those medieval tourists, the "palmers" who had already made the big pilgrimage to Jerusalem and returned with their palm frond souvenirs, even they seek *straunge strondes,* shores as far afield as they can manage. It's deep, this instinct to move. And never satisfied.

But if leisure (the leisure that promotes *the life of the mind*) is what's missing from our overamped world, if the rich multitasked life is the problem, shouldn't a person stay put, lie low?

This is the dilemma, my dilemma, maybe an essential contemporary middle-class dilemma: To stay? Or to go? Be Pascal? Or be Chaucer?

If you're a "seeker" (and who, opening a book, is not?), isn't the open road the only way, paradoxically, to find the lost life of daydream where all the rest—wisdom, decency, generosity, compassion, joy, and plain honesty—are sequestered?

If life *is* a journey, has it just become a getaway to somewhere warm on JetBlue? How to be a pilgrim without being either a tourist or, worse, a pious trekker, lugging freeze-dried soup on your back, believing it's all about "getting away"— especially from other people?

Not my problem. I don't want to get away from anyone. I want someone back. But that can't happen.

What would it be like to believe we'd meet again, he and I? Heaven, life after life—one trip I can't imagine. The beautiful hand that held mine all those years—gone. Gone for good (strange phrase—what's good about it?). Dust now. Ashes, in fact, but the biblical word insists—*for dust thou art, and unto dust shalt thou return,* as if to make the point: we're not simply reduced to our burnt leftovers. We return to the earth, become the anonymous stuff of the planet.

To travel to get away from absence—that's more like it. Not to get away from someone or anyone. Not even to get away from sadness (the sweet melancholy that makes so much poetry), though maybe to avoid the kindly pity so generously offered.

The road, then, not the room.

Back to the notebooks, the stash I've been adding to methodically, like a retirement fund building all these years, a diverse portfolio of growth stocks, many of them collapsed to nothing (Cioran—out! Even Marcus Aurelius, once such a strong contender, strikes me now as a tedious bluffer).

There, winking from one notebook to another, but mostly ignored and unquoted, popping up now like a friend I keep meaning to reestablish contact with, is the boy *with bold ideas and opinions beyond his years,* followed up the sixteenth-century château staircase by his lute player. Michel Montaigne, *sluggish, lax, drowsy.*

This is the writer, midway between Chaucer's pilgrimage in the fourteenth century and Kafka's reclusiveness in the twentieth, who chooses to sit in a cold stone tower and see what will roll or writhe his way.

Yet Montaigne reports that he is most alive on his horse, galloping on the road in all weathers. *I don't portray being. I portray passing.* He doesn't mean the passage of eras, of history, its long broken arc. He means movement "minute to minute," the inner tick-tock of thought. He means he portrays—paints is the added meaning of the word in French—what passes through the mind. His own.

Follow him then, the first modern. So go. And also—stay.

To Go

Programmed for pilgrimage, squeezing the lemon of location for all it's worth, looking for meaning, the last drop left over from the lived life of others. Location, location, location, as if life were fundamentally a real estate transaction.

My own life list, as birders say of their sightings, is long. Freud's house at Berggasse 19 in Vienna? Been there, wrote it up. Leaving the flat, annoyed that the effort of finding the building (it was not yet on the tourist track) hadn't been worth the trouble. Then, pausing on the clammy staircase, dark moss and springy lichen in the shadowy corner, the dart of realization, the sensation that *just here,* on the turn of the stone landing, his patients must have stopped too, pivoting from the session back into their real (or feigned) lives. I had stumbled, I felt sure, on the locus of many revelations.

Later, I tracked The Couch to Hampstead. But he wasn't there. The landing outside the Vienna flat was where he was to be found, head turned away, white hair thinning, faint

odor—a chewed cigar, but of course it was just the sodden
scent of rain from earlier in the day.

Closer to home, a road trip to Iowa to find Dvořák, wandering around the Turkey River, tiny tributary of the Mississippi, to visit the Czech-settled farm town of Spillville where
he spent the summer of 1893. Hoping to hear, as he had, the
scarlet tanager drilling the motif of the scherzo of the *American Quartet*. Didn't find the bird, but, amazingly, found
Dvořák. A stump by the Turkey River where he sat, listening,
getting the local boys to flush birds for him. His pretty daughter Otilka fancied a Kickapoo drummer—that was the end of
the family's unlikely summer in Iowa. I sussed a book out of
that too.

Another time, another "project," off to Greece and Turkey
"in the footsteps of Saint Paul," as I wrote in the proposal for a
travel grant. Went there to find the narrative for a book. But I
decided, after all, to leave Paul to the scholars, and wrote
nothing, asking the guide as we drove on and on in the little
top-heavy van, from Tarsus to Antioch, along the eastern
Mediterranean from Iconium to Perga, on to Ephesus, "Did
Paul walk all this?" *Yes, all this, 100 percent for sure.* Hours
later, still in the van, the dun-colored dust coating the glass
rectangle I looked out, the crunch of stone when the tires
veered to the edge: "And this whole way too?" *Yes, I tell you, all
this, on foot, all this, 100 percent for sure.* I closed my eyes,
curled up in my seat, flummoxed by such zeal, glad of the AC.

The Galilee? Made that trip too, against the advice of the
fretful (*Isn't that near the Golan Heights? Do you think you
should . . . ?*). Believe it or not, Jesus was there, Lake Kinneret

smooth as a rink that June afternoon, easily walkable. A boat set off in the distance, *slap, slap,* the distant sound of fisher-folk, as if a figment of Minnesota's wild rice waterways had followed me to that arid place. Always at home near a fishing lake.

He had not been in Jerusalem amid the smoky votive lights of the Armenian watchdogs of the sepulcher. But I should not have been surprised to find him on the pristine shores near Capernaum. Nor was this a Christian theme park. It seemed untouched. Timeless. His.

Oh no, said the Catholic priest who was showing me around. *Oh no, the Israelis would never let anyone junk this up—it provides a big percentage of the drinking water for the country.*

Sacred water because secular water. An even better miracle these days than water into wine—water into water. Liked that. But for some reason I never wrote up that agreeable irony, except in my notebook, the slag heap of the annotated life tossed along paths abandoned or never taken. Honestly wasted moments, as so many details deserve to be, even when they are given their humble habitation on the private page. Let them get lost in their unnumbered diary pages.

There is, as well, an even longer list of saints I sought—a bus from Paris to Lisieux to find the tubercular Carmelite, Thérèse, author of the first autobiography of my girlhood, sending showers of roses from heaven after her death at twenty-four. I took hers for my confirmation name—Patricia Mary Thérèse, mainly for the Frenchy accents. I fostered a taste for youthful death, and dreamed of going to Lima to see the bed of broken bricks Saint Rose slept on in a hut behind her family's grand mansion, a life of ardent denial. All the jewels—rubies, sapphires—she refused to wear. Her furious father. That trip never happened, my *Lives of the Saints* period petered out before I achieved Latin America.

But I made it to Assisi for Francis, the best saint of them all—he got a whole book from me. The following year, off to England to Norwich for Saint Julian, the anchoress confined to her little cell, a carbuncle stuck on the side of the Church of Saint Julian (hence her name—no one really knows who she was, she with her mystic visions). Julian and her sole companion, a little cat who is always at her feet in pictures and statuary, the tail neatly rounding his upright body. The "showings" came to her in fits, and then, convalescing, she wrote them down. T. S. Eliot quotes her at the end of *Four Quartets,* as if her fourteenth-century assurance that *all shall be well, all manner of thing shall be well* could assuage the savage wounds of the twentieth.

Then, naturally enough, on to Anne Frank—up early, ahead of everyone that cold spring morning in Amsterdam, I was the first to lumber up the narrow staircase, getting the room to myself for five minutes before the world crowded in behind me, mostly schoolchildren on a field trip.

I hardly realized all these trips were pilgrimages, sometimes spiritual, more often secular, hajjes to the homes or haunts of figures I knew—or felt I knew, people who flared alive in my mind from reading. They seemed to invite me from the page to call on them, as if they were *there*, a trace at least. A literary bloodhound on the prowl not for ghosts, but for leftover life. Evidence. Of what? History? Evidence of the combustible urgency of the soul?

But then, what *is* travel but a search for what has preceded us—a personage, a habitation. Whitman was wrong about that—the open road isn't open. At least it isn't vacant. Even a hike or canoe trip into wilderness that seems to be outside history, repudiating human narrative, even such travel is a search for *before*—the trace of an ancient tree, Precambrian rock, rare ladyslipper orchid in a reclusive swamp. The pristine location sought by the naturalist is a figment of time immemorial. Virgin history before we made up History. But history, nonetheless.

The first time I went to England, after graduate school, I had to remind myself: *There will be cars, skyscrapers, fast food.* My England was a set design by Jane Austen, George Eliot, and my great favorite, Thackeray. Literature had been my Elsewhere long before I left St. Paul. In London that first trip, I choked on a nut sandwich in a vegetarian teashop built into William Blake's house, and had time to think, before someone smacked me on the back and I was saved—*Jeez, I'm dying where Blake wrote his poems.*

In time, writers overtook the saints, and became a different canon—Katherine Mansfield in Bandol, Hemingway at his standing desk in Key West, all those cats catting around. Then Hampstead again, this time for Keats, also Guy's Hospital for him, and finally, as he did, off to Rome, the little room overlooking the Spanish Steps where he died, tourists in shorts and cartoonish running shoes lined up on the steps eating ice cream, an American undergrad laughing to his buddy, leaping past the window of the bedroom, taking the steps two at a time, yelling *fuck, no! fuck, man!*

Later to Amherst for Emily Dickinson's house and the gravesite—*Called Home*. Along the Promenade in Brooklyn for Whitman, reading "Crossing Brooklyn Ferry." And a blistering hot July afternoon in the cool library of Indiana University for Sylvia Plath's baby book—her mother's itty-bitty control-freak handwriting telling you all you needed to know about where her frightful ambition was hatched.

I almost never travel for a vacation—I take off for commemorative or even funerary experience, as if all the world were a vast and not cheerless cemetery, the ghosts still murmuring if you can get close enough. Well, most of them, even the saints, were writers, so the words are audible as you move from room to room of their houses or through the gardens—Rye House garden for Henry James. I sweet-talked my way in there on a day when it was closed, taking the train from London. James was my hero of the notebook, not of the novel: *If one was to undertake to tell tales and to report with truth on the human scene,* he said in his wonderfully overstuffed way, *it could but be because notes had been from the cradle the ineluctable consequence of one's greatest inward energy . . . to take them was as natural as to look, to think, to feel, to recognize, to remember.* I sought out Rye House, pledging my allegiance to the note, the shard, the fragment, the bit that glints in the dirt and makes the book possible. I knew even then I didn't believe in the narrative arc, that fiction of fiction.

I've even contrived to live in a shrine myself—though I didn't plan it or realize it when I moved in years ago: Scott

Fitzgerald's St. Paul, his grandmother's slice of a witchy old row house in the old Cathedral Hill neighborhood, my home these last thirty-six years. It was a sad-sack crumbling place when I arrived, a heartbreak hotel without children or pets, housing an array of fixed-income tenants—a defrocked priest, the physician who'd lost his license but not his thirst for Canada rye, an array of maiden/divorced/widowed ladies (hard to tell the category of loneliness), one a woman who wondered if I would be interested in seeing a letter from Willa Cather she had received as a girl. Maybe it was worth something? Did I know? Not that she would ever part with it, *absolutely not*— as if I had asked to buy it. Astrology magazines came regularly for several of them, their only apparent mail.

I was surprised to find next door the retired "lay teacher" from my old high school. She taught Spanish, not my language: I belonged to France and Sister Peronne Marie, the cloistered nun who taught us how to use the Paris Métro from a grid she mimeoed and gave to each of us: *Girls, how do we get from Invalides to Marché aux Puces at Porte de Clignancourt? What are the transfer points?*

The old Spanish teacher greeted me warily, with shy hope as I lugged my boxes of books and not much else up to the second floor: *Do you like scotch, dear?*

Before long, the museum curators and the psychotherapists began buying up the old heaps—this is the neighborhood, in fact the very block, where Jonathan Franzen opens his novel *Freedom,* earnest young couples acquiring abandoned mansions for a song, ruining their marriages with too much infidelity and paint-stripping.

For all my gallivanting, I've never left. I'll get to that too. It's part of the love story, the beautiful hand that held mine. He had the apartment on the first floor as I trudged up to the second with my boxes of books. My girlfriend, helping me move, said excitedly, *There's the most interesting-looking man in the first-floor apartment—his door was open. Maybe you'll meet him* . . . The quotation is exact—strange that it imprinted itself, though I said, *Are you kidding?* I was just breaking up with a boyfriend. I wasn't looking for Mr. Right. I didn't believe there was such a person.

But there you are—the downstairs neighbor introducing yourself the next morning. Bright October, crisp and fresh. The City of St. Paul was planting a tree—a laurel tree— below my window just then. *I have a graduate degree in lyric poetry,* I thought. *I know a symbol when I see one: putting down roots.* I was holding a teacup, smiling, when there was the knock on the door. You. Would I like to be shown where the garbage bins were? The location was a little tricky, you said. I followed you into the alley, behind a rickety arbor fence, listened intently as you said the landlord required everything to be tied up in plastic bags. I was trying to think of something else I could ask you to tell me about.

So we began. The first cup of coffee. The new life within twenty-four hours of the old. The life now ended, the hand now dust. Dust, but it must be said, gold dust. Memory glints. The laurel tree is huge now, should be pruned, the bark cracked. But still alive.

Now high school students come to the building on assignment, snapping Instagrams to prove to their teachers that they've made the assigned circuit of the Fitzgerald locations. The "birth house" is three blocks up the street. It seems the English teachers insist on these pilgrimages, apparently more essential than reading the books. I often find a teenager on our staircase. More pilgrims, believers in the unreal estate of history-touched locations. I see I'm not alone in this.

So I'll make the rounds, take my notes (*the ineluctable consequence of one's greatest inward energy*) on a tour of the heroes of leisure, confined till now in my stack of notebooks, but out there, part of the great world. I'm ready to roll: carry-on bag, Montaigne (all of him) on the iPhone. Off I go. Looking for ease—if not my own ease. That's gone, along with you. Reason enough to head out.

On the night of Monday, March 30, 1778, an Anglo-Irish lady named Sarah Ponsonby, age twenty-three, the un-married dependent of well-placed relatives (her parents long dead), slipped out of her guardians' Georgian mansion in Woodstock, Kilkenny, the rest of the house asleep. She was dressed in men's clothing, had a pistol on her, and carried her little dog, Frisk.

She made her way to the estate's barn where Lady Eleanor Butler, a spinster sixteen years her senior, a member of one of the beleaguered old Catholic dynasties of Ireland (the Dukes—later the Earls—of Ormonde), was awaiting her, having decamped from stony Butler Castle twelve miles dis-tant on a borrowed horse. She too was wearing men's breeches and a topcoat.

Their plan, long schemed, was to ride through the night, the moon a bare sliver, to Waterford, twenty-three miles away on the coast, and from there to embark for England to live together somewhere (they had no exact destination) in "delicious seclusion." Their goal was "Retirement," a life of "Sentiment" and "Tenderness."

Their alarmed relatives followed in panicked pursuit, intercepting them in a barn where they had sheltered overnight when they missed the packet boat. It is thought they were given away by the frantic yapping of Frisk. They were hauled back to their respective homes, where Sarah, having caught a cold in the barn, advanced the plot of their gothic tale by falling seriously ill with fever.

Her life hung in the balance, but not her determination. The sweet-tempered, seemingly tractable Sarah told her guardians that were she denied her desire to "live and die with Miss Butler," such a refusal would, according to a correspondent of her distressed guardian Lady Betty Fownes, "provoke her to an act that would give her friends more trouble than anything she had yet done." A wiry will was coiled under her mild demeanor, betraying a capacity to perform acts more bold than the purse crocheting she was known for in the Fownes's salon.

As Sarah recovered over the next month, she and Lady Eleanor wore down their dismayed relatives. Everyone was comforted that at least "there was no man concerned with either of them," as Lady Betty put it with some relief, if deeper perplexity.

Finally, with the two families apparently played out by the intransigence they faced, the two friends were allowed to leave Ireland together on a lovely May morning in a fashion less romantic but more commodious than their attempted escape some weeks before—they were provided with a coach to the seaport and were accompanied by a Butler housemaid, Mary Carryll. It was reported they were laughing merrily as they stepped into the coach.

The plot was yet richer. Sarah Ponsonby's guardian, Sir William Fownes, had confessed his passion for her in the midst of the upheaval. He entreated her, down on his knee, to stay in Kilkenny. He had been rather counting on Lady Betty's poor health to release him before long. Thinking himself something of a catch (he was just over fifty and allowed that he considered himself to have "a pretty face"), he still hoped to provide a male heir to the family baronetcy (poor Lady Betty having managed only a daughter, now grown and married with children of her own in Dublin). Sarah Ponsonby had come into the household thanks to Betty, her kindhearted elder cousin who had taken in the orphan girl, originally against the grumpy objections of the later smitten Sir William.

Lady Betty seems to have been exhausted by the romantic upheaval of it all. Her response to her husband's passion and Sarah's horrified rebuff was to leap over all these unruly emotions and head straight for the comforts of the grave, writing her "dear Sir Wm" a letter without a note of outrage or betrayal, outlining her burial wishes with housewifely economy:

> *I have always ment to be a good Wife and Mother and hope you think Me so. As to my Funeral I hope youl allow me to be Buried as I like, which is this: When the Women about me are sure I am dead, I would be Carried*

to the Church and kept out of Ground two days and
nights, four Women to sitt up with me. . . . No body to
be at My Funeral but my own poor, who I think will be
sorry for me.

Lady Betty proved to be prescient, though her order backwards: while the Ladies were touring Wales, looking for a
place to retire in delicious seclusion, Sir William succumbed
to a stroke, though not before he was "cup'd blistered and
glistered" in the medical method of the day. As he feared, the
family baronetcy was extinct with his death.

Lady Betty, with her weak heart, soon followed. They were
buried side by side in the little Church of Ireland graveyard
near their Woodstock home. Lady Eleanor and Sarah Ponsonby, careering around the countryside near the river Dee,
looking for their ideal retreat, were blissfully unaware of this
sad Irish epilogue to their own happy Welsh ending. Or their
beginning, as it proved to be.

The "Ladies," as they were known in Llangollen, and are
known still (for of course I went there), settled themselves
and proceeded to pass fifty years in their "Welsh vale," living
the hyperdomesticated "retirement" they had dreamed of in
Ireland.

They soon became celebrated. They were famous for wishing to be left alone.

In pursuing the Ladies in Llangollen, I was not *discovering*
them, though no one I mentioned them to had heard of them.

I was picking up a trail first laid down by their intrigued contemporaries two centuries earlier. During the Ladies' long years in their home, called Plas Newydd, it seems just about everyone beat a path to the heavily ornamented Gothic door of their remote "Cottage." Wordsworth and Southey composed poems under its low roof; both Shelley and Byron turned up to talk and "stare," apparently flummoxed by the orderly cloister life of the Ladies. Charles Darwin came as a child in the company of his father; Lady Caroline Lamb (the novelist and lover of Lord Byron—and a distant relative of Sarah) made a visit. As did Sir Walter Scott. Even the Duke of Wellington (a treasured friend) and De Quincey ("coldly received")—on and on the personages of the age made pilgrimage to the isolated Welsh village on the river Dee. Josiah Wedgwood visited the Ladies to tour and opine about the rock formations of the surrounding "savage" landscape.

"The two most celebrated virgins in Europe" became, with their pastoral life, both a model and a curiosity. The poet Anna Seward, known as "the Swan of Litchfield," visited and corresponded with the Ladies. Various royals from the Continent also made the pilgrimage—the aunt of Louis XVI, Prince Esterházy from Budapest. Coming and going, the aristocrats paid wistful (or baffled) homage to a way of life rare in its independence and chosen affection.

Some visitors spent the night at Plas Newydd, though this was not favored by the reclusive Ladies, who valued their quiet nights à deux, tucked up by the fire (made up by Mary Carryll), reading aloud to each other from French novels. They directed visitors to put up at the Hand, the Llangollen inn still open for business today in a wan sort of way, a big barny hotel where, a sign indicates, the Llangollen Rotary Club meets every Monday, 5 p.m., save for bank holidays.

The Ladies called on the Hand when they needed to hire a coach. But Eleanor and Sarah rarely required a coach—they stayed home. That was the point, or part of their point. The retired life was the cloistered life. Secular nuns.

No wonder I begin my not very leisurely tour of leisure with them. *You and your nuns!* he used to say, charmed in his amused non-Catholic way by my "nun thing." He loved to call out in mock horror from the living room if I was in the kitchen—*Oh no,* The Nun's Story *is on Public TV again tonight!*

Cue my reply: *I have three words for you, mister—Super Bowl Sunday.*

All the ways we contrived, over the years, over all the differences, to say *crazy about you, just crazy about you.*

Within five years of their taking up residence in Llangollen, the Ladies' renown was so far advanced that the queen was asking to see the plans of their cottage and garden. The plans were lost—or perhaps discarded: Queen Charlotte was known to abhor the scent of musk, the very perfume the Ladies lavished on their linens and all correspondence sent from Plas Newydd. Anything posted from the Cottage was redolent of their signature funky fragrance. But in spite of the musk, the word from those who visited was that the Cottage and environs were beguiling—and the Ladies themselves "enchantresses."

Llangollen is hardly a straight shot from London, even to-day. It might have been easier to hire a coach in the eigh-teenth century to visit the Ladies at Plas Newydd. I used public transport, not trusting my American self to drive on the left side of the road without him in the passenger seat saying without alarm *left, darling, left,* when (not if) I made a turn into the right lane.

After the train from London Euston to Chester (two hours), a branch line train to a place called Ruaton that appeared to be an abandoned station. The next step was a bus. Where was that? No one around to ask. I lugged my roller bag across the railroad overpass, and wandered out to a roadway, overjoyed to see a bus stop a block up the way with a weather-beaten sign. Cars (not many) went by, a truck or two. Finally, the bus.

And was told I was standing on the wrong side of the road for the bus to Llangollen. *Opposite side, luv.* It felt like a time warp, merrie olde England, cuppa tay, though this was Wales. The road signs were in Welsh (bigger) and English (under-neath), as if to make clear what mattered in these parts.

It was late afternoon by the time I got to Llangollen, the bus dropping me by the river on the edge of the action. Ca-sino, hotels offering teas, B&Bs to the left, hotels to the right. A tourist town—not because of the Ladies. I seemed to be alone in coming to the little town on the river Dee to find them. Hiking, biking, whitewater rafting, a steam train chug-ging along an otherwise abandoned track to be had for an af-ternoon outing, canal boats and horse-cart rides. Families and young cyclists streaking by in the eely skintight garments they wear, and their reverse number, retired couples (not the soulful retirement the Ladies sought) on modest walking tours, lumbering along, stopping for afternoon cake, drinks before the beef dinner. Or up to the romantic ruins of Valle Crucis (the outing the Ladies sometimes undertook with their visitors).

I had a reservation at a hotel I had chosen for the name—the Falls, assuming it must overlook the river, picking up on Josiah Wedgwood's fascination with the area's wild land-scape. It soon became evident I should have chosen the Cornerstone, directly across the street: it had the river view.

The entry door of the Falls was locked, the attached wine bar closed. I bumped my roller bag across to the Cornerstone. It looked like an illustration for *The Old Curiosity Shop,* mullioned windows, dark interior.

In a trice, fairytale fast, the door was opened by the owner, who introduced herself as Carol—*C'min, c'min, cold as winter, hardly any kind of June day.* She took charge of the roller bag and me. *You'll want tea. Taste for cake?* I was told to sit by the fire. And fell into a voluminous sofa, deep with oversize pillows. I'm not sure what a peat fire is, but I think this was a peat fire, the smell of something danker than a wood log, heavy with compounded forest. Lap of comfort, if not luxury. Tea and a hard little cake (*meant to be dipped—dip it, my dear!*) arrived on a tray, milk, demerara sugar cubes, thin paper napkin.

Did Carol know about the Ladies? Oh yes, quite the pair, they.

As for the owner of the Falls, she did not wish to speak ill—neighbor, friends across the divide, all that—but well, where was he? Allowing herself a professional shrug—what do you expect? Didn't live on the premises. She lived on the premises.

Unfortunately, the Cornerstone was entirely booked—pity.

I felt a stab of disappointment, as if the Ladies, who had brought me all this way, had cozied up together by their peat fire, reading *La Nouvelle Héloïse* to each other, and then dispatched me to the Hand.

I was nicely settled in by the Cornerstone fire when the owner of the Falls (located on his cell phone by Carol) arrived on the sidewalk and put his face to the mullion. The little square window filled with his big head. He spotted me in the cheerful dark dipping my brittle cake into the milky tea. In he bounded. It was my fault, somehow, that I had not located him—not that it mattered, he said. *Come along then.* A nod to Carol, and we were off. She wouldn't accept payment for the tea. *Glad to take in a stray, come anytime.* It was raining now, the owner blustering across the street. *Come along.*

My room was on the third floor of an old building, many coats of stucco whited over. Narrow staircase, the roller bag bumping behind me, the room larger than I expected, with a sloping floor, double bed, the mattress cratering toward the center, everything clean and orderly, dried flowers, only slightly dusty, on the mantel of the fireplace (*no, no, entirely bricked up, no fires here, I'll tell you*). It was the tatty look I remembered from my first trips to England in the 1970s (Keats, Blake, Wordsworth). Décor meant to convey hominess, but experienced as dispiriting.

Too bad I was missing the wine bar, the owner was saying. Best wine bar in town, he didn't mind claiming. But closed Sundays. Try the Corn Mill, he suggested, and pointed the way. *Bit of a trek in the rain, but who's afraid of a little damp, there you go.*

The Corn Mill was a stylish place fitted into (what else?) an abandoned stone corn mill, "repurposed" as a restaurant overlooking the Dee. Bar downstairs, mostly young people, loud and happy. Upstairs in the quiet restaurant I found a corner table with a small window to myself, almost as cozy as the Cornerstone by the peat fire with my tea and cake. I looked down at the river billowing with mist, the rain steady now, the night lowering. Imagine Eleanor and Sarah arriving about the same time of year. Spring can be cold, the rain penetrating. No wonder they loved their fire. Strangers here, but not, at least, alone.

Why is it still so hard to enter a restaurant on my own, take a table, settle in to the business of dinner, as if eating alone were faintly reprehensible? My mother's voice homing in as I lie under Mr. Kinney's beechnut tree. *Well, it's sad, darling—he drinks alone.* And me, waiting for a glass of wine.

It's a feminist thing—I know, I know. I've read the articles in the women's magazines, how you must walk right in, take possession—and don't let them park you next to the kitchen door.

The woman who dines alone. The postmodern valor I struggle to claim. I've never had this anxiety about traveling alone, which I've done for years. But the barricade of a good restaurant for dinner (lunch, strangely, poses no problem)—

for that I must suit up. The armor covering my unease is always a book tucked in my purse, as if I packed a pearl-handled pistol. More recently, the iPhone. But somehow a book seems more companionable. I put it on the table to my right, security detail, riding shotgun.

The waiter arrives, sweet kid with a concerned look. He brings me my glass of wine, still frowning. Something bothering him. Maybe I shouldn't have seated myself? *No, no, not that at all, madam.*

He would like to see me at a better table, the larger table by the big window with what he thinks—what he knows (*Been here all my life, haven't I?*)—has the better view. Big storm coming, lightning and that, something to see. I argue for my small table with the partial river view, and try to foist off concern for him as a reason to stay put: won't he need the big table when the place starts to fill up?

He insists on being the feminist—*You're a nice lady and you got here first, didn't you?* He wins. Picks up my wineglass, settles me and my book at the big table with the big window, and goes off, much relieved that things are now as they should be.

The place did fill up. I held uneasily to my fiefdom with the best river view as couples and larger groups mounted the stairs, gazing around for a good table, lowering an eye at me with my lamb (*The best thing on our menu, if I may suggest . . .*); the second glass of wine, my low-grade misery, my difficulty claiming my place on planet earth.

I open my book, which is meant to prove I'm sustaining a relationship of some kind like everybody else out for the night. I'm dining with Colette.

I discovered the Ladies from her. I'm rereading the chapter she devotes to them in *The Pure and the Impure,* the book she considered her best, "the nearest I shall come to writing an autobiography." Two of Colette's biographers, I've read elsewhere, seem uneasy about the book being her "best," saying it displays a certain "incoherence" (Joanna Richardson), and the prose is rather "cryptic" (Judith Thurman).

In this book about the first stirrings of modernity and Colette's revisitation of her gallant cross-dressing, lipstick lesbian youth, the Ladies seem oddly placed. They get a whole long chapter. Strange to find them here. Once again, as they were in the eighteenth century, Lady Eleanor and Sarah are outliers, conscripted this time into a tour of early-twentieth-century escapades from Colette's years as a "vagabond," her jaunty term for her youthful transgressive self.

The book's other chapters are portraits from Colette's fin de siècle experiences, observations of the lives of those living on the wild side of desire at the cusp between the belle epoque and modernism when the demimonde was not, as it has since become, pretty much the monde entire. The book does not strike me as particularly autobiographical, at least not in the self-revealing way we expect now of memoir. Much of the fan-dancing is performed well behind the fan.

The Wikipedia entry for the book describes it as a "novel," as do some of the readers posting responses online. Yes, I'm online. My waiter has given me the restaurant's Wi-Fi password, so I'm dining not only with Colette but with any number of people who have opinions about her and much else. Is it really possible that Kobe Bryant has posted a Goodreads rating of *The Pure and the Impure*? Three stars. A man of few words: "What I've learned is that when the Goodreads description says 'erotic,' it never is." Kobe Bryant? There he is—or someone claiming to be Kobe Bryant—and mightily disappointed in Colette.

I'm heartened that Kobe Bryant confirms my thoughts. *The Pure and the Impure* isn't a novel, nor is Colette a "reporter" as she suggests in the opening pages. The book is rich in her signature descriptive riffs, revisiting scenes and people from a life now at a distance, looking them up in memory to see if they have anything further to report on the ever-beguiling subject of desire, festooning scenes with volleys of dialogue as if she had a tape recorder in her pocket all those years ago.

But what are the Ladies doing here? On this, Kobe has nothing to say. All the figures Colette describes come from her world and observation—except Eleanor and Sarah. They belong to that other history—History—the past beyond memory.

The book isn't an autobiography, and the Ladies' chapter isn't quite a work of history. There is nothing to call research, and of course no "reporting." Instead, speculation. And assumption. Or presumption.

The Pure and the Impure opens with a memory of a visit to an opium den where Colette claims the identity of journalist. She tells her host she is "here on professional assignment," giving herself the ideal narrative cover—observer, not participant: she doesn't take the offered pipe, the pinch of cocaine. This refusal is emblematic of Colette's teasing tour of the *banlieues* of desire that follows. The source of the book's "cryptic prose" seems to be the feinting and lunging Colette performs throughout about her own sexuality.

It is strange that she should invite readers to call this now-you-see-me-now-you-don't book her nearest try at autobiography. But then, maybe foregrounding life's sinkholes and silences *is* the deepest resolve of autobiography, and not, as we tend to think, confession, display, self-revelation.

The book is a scattering of prose patches held loosely together by the notion of the power of the senses. Montaigne again—the book along the lines of "these things" that Montaigne, loath to be corralled into form, called his basket of thoughts and observations. Maybe such random takes on a subject, barely held together by the idea of a chapter and certainly not comprising anything as taut as narrative, are the real destination of autobiography—not our experience as it is reeled out in stories, but the play of consciousness over the inchoate field of existence. What holds Colette's "things" together, if anything does, is the conundrum at their core: what is desire and why does it rule us?

Maybe, I decide, Colette abandons any pretense of autobiography or reportage and turns to the more distant region of History to grasp a life she can fashion into something more complete than a vignette, more than a shard of observation fitted into her collage of desire.

She not only conscripts the Ladies out of the eighteenth century and out of their Welsh cottage. She plunges forward, imagining them out of their century and into hers in 1930:

They would own a car, wear dungarees, smoke cigarettes, have short hair, and there would be a liquor bar in their

apartment. . . . Eleanor Butler would curse as she jacked
up the car, and would have her breasts amputated.

Anything amiss? The attentive lad who thinks I'm a nice lady deserving of the better view has returned. *Unhappy with the lamb?* I realize I've been scowling. At Colette. I've put down my fork and picked up my pen. In the margin, bearing down hard, next to the amputated breasts: *Puh-leeze.*

He clears my plate, inquiring if I might like the pudding. I remind myself this doesn't mean chocolate custard. It's how they say dessert over here—the upper classes insisting on the nursery word. Only the working classes say *dessert* in an effort to sound cultivated—this I've been told by an English friend. But he has turned it around again, the working lad who has picked up the way the nice ladies talk. I say, in my flat midwestern voice, *Thanks, yes, I'd like dessert.* It's tiramisu, he murmurs as if tending an irksome patient.

And the strongest coffee you have. I want something bitter. Off he goes.

I'm back with Colette and my annoyance. She feels free to make the Ladies into her cartoon—they're beyond living memory, beyond witnessing. How amusing—to be born in the eighteenth century with all its rules and regs, when in the twentieth century they could be free to tinker with a car and lop off their breasts. If they'd only lived in the twentieth century, the Ladies could have set up frankly as lesbians. For weren't they two women who so desired to be together, merge and love and entwine themselves, that they fled family and friends on the heroic wings of Eros?

Well, no. They *said* they didn't elope for this reason—even the word "elopement" did not have the erotic undertow in the eighteenth century that it has in ours. But of course we think we know better. We know what they were really up to because, in plucking them out of their moment in space-time and "understanding" them into our own, we see they were lesbians, never mind what *they* said.

I seem to be annoyed not only with Colette, but with the frame of mind I have inherited along with her—the postmodern pride of calling things by their names, the arrogance of assuming integrity is a matter of being more and more *open*. Or simply that a label, firmly affixed, is honesty in the face of euphemism and discretion. Why can they not be believed? Why must our age out them? They wanted to live the life of the mind, the life of perfection. Don't they get to say what they were up to?

Your voice again as I mutter inwardly to Colette. You're saying again with that amused affection, *You and your nuns . . . cool your jets, sweetheart.*

Stop it, darling. I'm investigating the desire for the cloister, not the bedroom—I think the Ladies were too. I'll never convince anyone of this, not Colette, not even you. Not in our age. But thanks anyway—thanks again and always—for making me laugh one more time.

After the half-eaten tiramisu (pudding after all, I realize) and the depth charge of black coffee, I leave a ridiculously outsize tip to confirm my bona fides as a nice lady. Then it's back up from the river under the owner's sagging umbrella, in the rain and gloom to the Falls, in the back door as the owner instructed. I seem to be the only one on "the premises," noticing lights on in the upper floors of the Cornerstone, though the ground floor where I sat by the peat fire is dark. Carol, surely, is up there, cup of tea or "something stronger" (she had offered that in the afternoon).

Up to my room, propped against all the pillows on the sagging bed across from the yawning decorative fireplace and dusty former flowers, I swap out *The Pure and the Impure* for the biography of the Ladies (they finally got one a generation after Colette). Honest research, years of steadfast sleuthing, careful footnotes, many visits to the sites, full index at the back. A writer to trust—Elizabeth Mavor. In the acknowledgments, she thanks for their gracious help the staff of Plas Newydd—where I go tomorrow.

Up early, but Plas Newydd doesn't open for several hours. It's still raining, the sky heavy, sodden. This isn't going to blow over.

Then back along the street to the café overlooking the falls that are rushing, thanks to the rain. Lashings of milky Assam in a clattery cup and saucer. My notebook open, paging around to see what's there before I describe the weather, always my starter in the morning. Here's Pavarotti copied from an interview somewhere: *One of the very nicest things about life is the way we must regularly stop whatever it is we are doing and devote our attention to eating.* A leisure man.

I take the hint and order a big stunner of a breakfast, then head back to the Falls and the cratering bed and sink into something deeper than a nap. I awaken an hour later, fever-ish, hungover from a bacon and eggs bender.

Still too early to walk to Plas Newydd. I've finished Eliza-beth Mavor's biography of the Ladies, so I turn back to Mon-taigne, as if he were—well, he is—the real destination, held in reserve, but always there, shadowing me, beckoning deeper into whatever the idea of "retirement" has to offer. I tap on the iPhone to the Audible version of *The Complete Essays,* earbuds plugged in. The British voice reads to me, the voice my midwestern ear can't help hearing as . . . snooty. It is not at all how I hear the *Essais* when I read them myself, marking the margins.

Not that Montaigne's voice in my reading ear is modern or breezy or that I would want that kind of louche contemporary voice reading to me. Impossible to imagine Montaigne con-fining himself to 140 strokes of a dip pen. His formality is part of his age, a world that accepted the primacy of the com-plex clause, the sprung coil of thought releasing itself in a long periodic sentence. The page is an open prairie he rides across (he claimed to like riding even more than writing).

If there is an agenda in the *Essais,* it is his determination to be nobody but himself. Whoever that is. That's the point—to write in order to be a self to himself. In particular, he is wary of sounding—or being—scholarly, especially of sound-ing literary. *Ainsi, lecteur, je suis moy-mesmes la matière de mon livre.* So, reader, I am myself the material—the stuff—of my book.

He can't help making this pledge not to himself, but to "the reader." The reader, of course, is another version of the writer self. Montaigne speaks—all essayists do—with a personal voice but into an unknown, anonymous ear. Yet that other self—the reader—is also personal, intimate, individual, and has to be imagined out of oneself, not from someone else.

Though it occurs to me with one of those stabs of recognition I'm getting used to, I did have a reader. Across the yellow kitchen table all those years together. I handed over my drafts, and down he descended into himself, a concentration beyond me, past domestic life, even beyond our erotic life, into a pure and independent reader self, while I paced around, walked the dog, pretended not to be waiting for The Word. Pitch perfect, that ear of his. *On page 4, I wonder if you really mean . . .*

Montaigne says in "On Cannibals" (an *essai* I keep going back to) that he would strip naked before you (the reader) if doing so would get his meaning across more exactly. Across the centuries you can feel this is not a metaphor. Nakedness is truth.

It was for us, him and me. Of course that's how it started, naked and mad-happy—all those years ago. Back of the car at a rest stop—we did that all those years ago. Crazy to think of that—"all those years ago" as distant and yet immediate as "back of the car at a rest stop." A phrase that keeps drumming in my head—*all those years,* as if the accumulation of time should assure endurance, even immortality. Crazy how the mind works, chews really, on the one certainty—nakedness of body, of mind, of heart. Nakedness may be truth, but it's not immortality. As I keep thinking with a kind of awe—his beautiful hand, dust now. I seem to have fastened on his hand. As if thinking about it, *seeing* it with the narrow gold ring that meant he belonged to me, could conjure him entire.

Montaigne longed for naked utterance. He wanted, somehow, to let impulse dart around, then pin the butterfly of thought on the page. Not a tale or story, not an argument. A thought. Then another, another. Amounting to a collection. Or something even more gossamer than "a thought." He wanted to snare the *act* of thinking, consciousness shearing into articulation, a loose-moving cloud passing over the mind. *I don't portray being, I portray passing.* That movement might, after all, be the elusive self, the *moy-mesmes* he said was the stuff of his book.

In order to be trustworthy, writing must have a chaotic charge, an unbidden quality. The ease of passion—remember? Montaigne's kind of writing, anyway, had to have that:

> *If it doesn't go along gaily and freely, it goes nowhere worth going. We say of certain works that they smell of oil and the lamp, because of a certain harshness and roughness that labor imprints on productions in which it has a large part. But besides this, the anxiety to do well, and the tension of straining too intently on one's work, put the soul on the rack, break it, and make it impotent; as happens with water, which because of the very pressure of its violence and abundance cannot find a way out of an open bottle-neck.*

Like the Ladies, two centuries after him, Montaigne had "retreated." It's because of him I'm on the road, looking for those who believed, against the world's insistence on the value of labor, that leisure is what really matters in this life. My favorite sin of the Seven Deadly—sloth.

Except that isn't the word for this elusive quality, this golden time. Leisure isn't idleness, and it isn't simply an exhausted pause before shouldering the next task. I'm not just hunting down heroes of leisure for an eccentric little collection. I'm trying to figure out what it *is*, this leisure people now claim they do not have.

You're the last person to be talking about leisure—how often he said that when I started these trips, filling my notebooks. *You're a workaholic.* Always that amusement. And his encouragement—*Go ahead, off you go.* Always waiting for me when I came back. *Tell me what you discovered. You and your nuns. You and your subjects.*

Montaigne wanted to get away from the smell of oil and the lamp. Away from *the anxiety to do well.*

Know it well—the anxiety to do well. *You're the last person to talk about leisure. You're a workaholic, darling.*

The Ladies don't quote Montaigne. His name is not in Elizabeth Mavor's meticulous index. I'd been hoping to find him there. If Montaigne is the patron saint of modern leisure, surely the Ladies are its Enlightenment votaries. If he's the rock star of ease, I expected them at least to be latter-day roadies. He and the Ladies retreating during ages of political mayhem, ages of terrible certainty, accompanied by certainty's henchman, ruthlessness. They saw, Montaigne and the

Ladies, the act of leaving the world's stage as the best way to attain balance, and beyond that to reach the self's greatest achievement—integrity. This retreat from "the world" was the way to avoid the evil of certainty. The malignant cells of certainty that create the monster of demagoguery.

Maybe the Ladies didn't read Montaigne—they who read French as easily as English (and more often, all those French novels). They were great admirers of Rousseau, but then Rousseau was famously critical of (jealous of?) Montaigne. "I had always laughed at the false naïveté of Montaigne," Rousseau says in claiming his own greater authenticity. To him, while "making a pretense of admitting his flaws," Montaigne "takes great care to give himself only amiable ones." Rousseau didn't understand. Some people can't help being charming. It's not an act, it's a form of native generosity, the first step toward empathy.

The sky cleared long enough for me to get started, walking on the winding roadway from the tourist center of town to Plas Newydd. I turned up a narrow street to reach the main road to the property, and passed a building wedged between two others. A royal blue metal historical plaque was riveted to the gray wall, reporting that this was the original Old Post Office "from coaching days." Here, the sign said, Lady Eleanor Butler and Sarah Ponsonby had stayed before leasing Plas Newydd. Farther along, I passed the churchyard where all three of them—the Ladies and Mary Carryll, their faithful domestic— are buried. I didn't turn in there. Saving that for later.

The walk up to Plas Newydd went along a road of brick houses built on the slant of the rise, back gardens overrun with early summer flowers wagging in the rain (it had started up again, stinging in a sharp wind), hedges and bushes that would benefit from pruning, a hairless dog looking glum behind a fence, a house needing paint, a general air of things having been let go. I saw no one, the only language I encountered a large hand-lettered sign, fixed to a dilapidated wooden fence: NO DOG FOULING.

A neighborhood of plastic buckets left out for watering, Wellies on the back stoop, a vaguely tended weediness to the little plots, the sense that here people did things for themselves—or left them undone. On a sunny day all this would look cheery. Even today, the sky glooming above, it brought to mind the word *modesty*. Even *decency*. Not poor, not rich, just middling—and content with that ordinariness.

The turn into the property of Plas Newydd left behind this haphazard middle-class modesty. The lawn, vast and severely manicured, suggested a daft *Alice in Wonderland* set design by Disney. A herd of elephantine topiaries crouched on the lawn, green bulbous potentates in possession of the expanse. This was the same view of the property in the print from the Ladies' time reproduced in Elizabeth Mavor's biography. Then it was a sweetly idealized pasture for sheep, hummocky and serene. No topiaries.

I made for the teashop in what had once been the coach house. The weather was not encouraging, the woman who brought me my tea said with regret, as if it were her fault. She might have been the mother of the young waiter at the Corn

Mill. Or sister to Carol at the Cornerstone with her tea and cake. She radiated the same fretful personal responsibility for my comfort.

She loaned me a giant orange umbrella when I paid for my ticket to tour the house and grounds. I went out past the alarming topiaries, feeling outsize myself with my massive umbrella. The crushed gravel walkway led to the formidable house—hardly a cottage. The building was sheathed in wood painted white over the original (and now invisible) dove gray stone. The whole thing had been laced up in the nineteenth century with a black-painted geometric oak carapace in a vaguely Elizabethan style suggesting half-timbering.

All this was the work of a series of owners after the Ladies' time, after another century of extension and redecorating, after a fire destroyed the expansion, followed by years of neglect and dry rot, until the property came into the possession of the local council, which had seen to the renovation in the final years of the twentieth century. Just in time.

Impossible to restore precisely the Ladies' Cottage as it had been in their time, given the centuries of overlay. But the lantern over the Gothic (Gothick, as the Ladies put it) doorway was theirs, as were the intricate black oak carvings of the little entry roof and the doorway I entered, handing my ticket to a boy sitting on a folding chair sheltering under a black umbrella. He jumped when I came around the turn to the entry, pulling the white cord of his iPod out of his ear.

How dark the place was. Yet once inside, there it was, the "Cottage" more or less reconstituted after all the expansions and extensions of wood had fallen victim to decay and neglect and fire. I stepped into the Gothick rooms they had known, their much-loved and fussed-over interior, the musk-scented stage for the life of retirement, their retreat from "every vexation." There was no musk, of course, only the faint fragrance of damp, the long vacancy of so many house museums. The odor not of death but of emptiness, the scent of life having decamped. This smell of absence, paradoxically, was heavy with presence.

I had the place to myself, turned to the right—main sitting room, dining room, surprisingly large kitchen. All of it shadowy, enclosed. Lady Eleanor saw to a well-provided table and a wine cellar of note. The Ladies were forever either in debt or in frenzied terror of ruin, waiting for Eleanor's family in Ireland to "settle" something substantial on them, or urging the Crown to provide a pension (for what? for being themselves, apparently).

They trembled with money worries, but kept on spending—on the gardens and the property, new shrubbery, the damming and redirection of the Cuffleyman, the "picturesque" stream that ran through the property. Nature often required an assist back to its ideal disorder. "Sat in the rustic seat," Eleanor wrote in her journal (a seat over the Cuffleyman she had of course *made* rustic), "disliked the appearance of the Stones over which the Water falls, thought it appeared too formal. Sent our workmen to it with a spade and Mattock."

Over the years, the Ladies found much to alter in nature's too great tidiness, much to decorate in the house interior, always discovering something that could be improved (or amplified or put in proper disarray). New doors for the library, a marble chimneypiece, carpets and curtains, upholstery. And a growing commitment to augmenting the grotesqueries of Gothick design, colored glass at the windows lending the place a cathedral air with images not of saints but suns and moons, stars, falcons, an antlered stag. The glass endures. I put my face to the white stag, looking out to the elephantine topiaries in the near distance. So much to ornament here in this paradise dedicated to the picaresque. Hard to say what the Ladies would make of the topiaries. Awfully formal. Then again, possibly Gothick at heart.

As for other expenses—a person had to eat, set a proper table, not to mention the occasional guests. When it was "Scowling and Black" outside in January, the Ladies were at table with roast goose and hog's puddings, though Eleanor's journal tut-tuts that they will "eat no more of the latter, too savoury, too rich for our abstemious Stomachs." Meals were a point of pride, or at least part of the rapturous daily accounting of the daily round of exquisite retirement. Lady Eleanor, always stocky, became quite stout. Even the wandlike Sarah filled out over the years. Clearly Pavarotti people, agreeing that *one of the very nicest things about life is the way we must regularly stop whatever it is we are doing and devote our attention to eating.*

They wore riding habits of black and men's top hats. They powdered their hair, a style long out of fashion. Much unkind merriment about their getups was made by visitors who saw them in their old age and found the riding habits and top hats absurd. But the local people thought them sensible, wearing outdoor clothes for a farm and garden life. They had their

uniform, and were free to ignore fashion, anticipating Gertrude Stein by over a century: "You can either buy clothes or
buy pictures," Hemingway quotes Stein as saying. "It's that
simple. No one who is not very rich can do both." Substitute
"buy shrubbery" for "buy pictures" and you have the essential
value at work here. Eleanor, vain about her journal and letter
writing, was happy to describe to a correspondent their excel-
lent larder, tended by Mary Carryll:

> *new laid Eggs from our Jersey Hens Who are in the Most*
> *beautiful Second Mourning you ever beheld . . . Dinner*
> *Shall be boil'd chickens from our own Coop. Asparagus*
> *out of our garden. Ham of our own Saving and Mutton*
> *from our own Village. . . . Supper Shall consist of Goos-*
> *berry Fool, Cranberry Tarts roast Fowel and Sallad.*
> *Don't this Tempt you.*

The Ladies' impulse for retreat, coupled with their compul-
sive tending of the Plas Newydd property, made them irre-
sistible outliers for an age just revving the engines of the
Industrial Revolution, whose speeded mass fabrication was
beginning to be mistrusted as a false new god laying waste
the pacific slowness of ages past. Among the genteel classes a
moist regret hovered over this pastoral ideal. This nostalgia,
like much nostalgia, was not for something actually experienced and lost, but for a notion held in the fond focus of the
imagination. "Retirement" was in the spirit of the times
among cultivated classes.

The Ladies were not alone in their pursuit of retreat, even if Dr. Johnson, cultural arbiter of the age, decried such fashionable rustication as "Civil suicide." He replied, famously and tartly, to James Boswell's question on the topic, "Why, Sir, you find no man, at all intellectual, who is willing to leave London. No, Sir, when a man is tired of London, he is tired of life; for there is in London all that life can afford." I had seen the *tired-of-London/tired-of-life* remark on tea mugs in souvenir shops near Big Ben.

This was the period when Marie Antoinette and her set were dressing up in faux farm frocks while she played shepherdess at her *hameau* at Petit Trianon, never imagining that barely a decade later she would be delivered to her beheading in a tumbrel, a farm cart whose usual purpose was for unloading manure in the fields.

There was a political echo of Montaigne's age in the Ladies' life as well—his age of Reformation and Counter-Reformation, wars and burned flesh, heads on pikes, and their age of the French Revolution and the subsequent Terror, another harvest of heads and body parts. Fevered certainties padding the way to unquestioned cruelties.

The French Revolution made the Ladies shudder— perhaps especially Catholic Eleanor, who had been educated by French nuns (*you and your nuns!*) at a convent boarding school in Cambrai, founded by a descendant of the martyred Sir Thomas More, a typical education for a Catholic aristo in Anglo-Ireland. Eleanor certainly would have heard of the murders (the martyrdoms) of Blessed Madeleine Fontaine and her small band of Sisters of Charity in June 1794 in

Arras, barely thirty miles from Cambrai. The nuns went to the guillotine singing the *Ave Maris Stella*.

But before the *déluge* of the Revolution, the Ladies shared with Marie Antoinette a taste for rural life—what they imagined and arranged for it to be. They took their cue from Rousseau. Lady Eleanor seems not to have carried her Catholicism from Ireland to Wales. But she harbored a Francophile soul of the ancien régime sort, including this passion for pastoral life.

Rustication was not simply chic. It presented itself as a saving grace against the dark satanic mills (Blake) and the getting-and-spending (Wordsworth) of the new world economic order. The world managed by academicians and technicians (business and markets, in a word) that we live in today is a souped-up version of the one the Ladies and their admirers saw with alarm rolling toward them and, they feared, soon rolling over them.

The Ladies lived to see France, whose language they knew and whose elegant humanist culture they revered, decimated by the Revolution and its bloody aftermath. They lived beyond that to see the further ruination of their orderly (well, feudal) values trashed by the usurper Napoleon. They did what they could to keep ordered grace going in their corner of Wales, chatelaines of serenity.

Yet theirs cannot be understood as a life of hedonism or even precisely of aestheticism. They had a daily regimen, as monastic orders always do, a strict rule of life. Their leisure, like a monastery's, was ruled by the clock. This domestic order may have been part of their "enchantment," why poets and nobles made the trek to their cottage door. They called their organized day *our System*. They were fearful of veering from it, as if the life of retirement relied, fundamentally and paradoxically, on discipline and strict observance, not indulgence. The System was the reason they never—almost never—left home. They had to obey the internalized bells of their ordered day, ringing its changes as it sent them about the business of their enclosure. Their devotions were not a prayer schedule, but acts of self-improvement, a vow of betterment for themselves and their patch of the world.

Each day was exactingly scheduled, hours given to study (languages especially: Italian, Spanish), transcription of admired texts, drawing and sketching, long walks, correspondence, reading, reading, reading in several languages—both silently and, at night, aloud to one another amid the glow of candles, an alarming expense of nine pounds per annum, but a requirement of the romantic reading life. Sarah ruined a map she was drawing one winter day and had to report in her diary that "a mistake in the Tropics has left me nothing to show for the last six weeks of my life."

I go up to the second floor, look at the vitrines displaying some of their possessions, the flowery tea set, the impossibly small embroidered satin pump (labeled as Eleanor's), the teeny-tiny "porcelain watering can the Ladies used to perfume their carpets." Droplets of musk sprinkled from the perforated spout.

Then down a couple dark steps to the woody box of the

dressing room where all the late-night reading amid the candlelight went on. So still. So silent.

So claustrophobic. I know I should spend longer in the house, take more notes, pause, conjure up the past. Conjure *them*. But I'm out the door, away from the dark Gothick fug of the place, past the boy listening to music (I can hear the ground beat) on his iPod.

I retrieve the big orange umbrella behind him, but keep it furled (the rain has stopped) and use it as a walking stick, poking the gravel as I make my way past the topiaries. No, I decide after all, Eleanor would send the workmen with their spades and mattocks to make the bombastic leafy beasts go away. Her Gothick was of the interior. Nature was meant to be wild—even if you had to train it to look wild.

I feel slightly elderly—or possibly I feel stately, moving forward with my walking stick, a woman of means surveying my domain. I'm headed toward the nature walk the Ladies loved, the "Home Circuit," what still exists of it, running along the Cuffleyman that rushes and burbles over the stones Eleanor often described in her journal as she did on a fine day in April 1788. The Ladies have taken their books into the garden, rising at six to an "enchanting morning." Their morning reading is Sterne. Wonderful to think of them reading *Tristram Shandy,* a novel that is a meandering bunch of narrative snippets and essays. Another writer belonging, if more narratively, to Montaigne's tribe.

Walking the Home Circuit, as they called this ramble from the house, past the pasture and gardens (no topiaries then), into the rough down by the Cuffleyman stream and its outcroppings, and back again, along the planted greenery they called their Shrubbery, to which they were ever adding and replanting.

"How splendid, how heavenly," Eleanor exults in her journal that day.

Then back inside "for a few Minutes to Write." For of course the retired life is the described life, the life relived in rolling sentences. Then out again with the letters of Madame de Sevigné to read in the rustic hut overlooking the Cuffleyman.

I have just arrived at the hut myself—the wood-roofed stone eyrie above the river that now has a sign directing visitors, in Welsh and English, with an arrow pointing the way through greenery and blossoming bushes—"Lady Eleanor's Bower." I have passed a bench or two, sequestered along the way, another little outbuilding across the Cuffleyman (several dainty bridges cross from one side to the other). But this is the place—wrought-iron gate, Gothick iron decorative medallions at the "windows" on the side opening to the Cuffleyman below. This was where they came on that perfect day in April 1788 to absorb (and radiate later in the journal) the sublime sensation of being alive.

"Such a day!" Eleanor reported. Then on to dinner at three: "roast breast of Mutton boil'd Veal Bacon and Greens Toasted Cheese."

All this was followed by "such a heavenly evening—blue Sky with patches of Cloud Scattered over it. So picturesque, like little Islands studding it." Back to the Shrubbery for another walk. Then on to the Bower where another sign, quite faded, reports what Eleanor records for the day in her journal: "Spent the Evening there. Brought our Books, planted out our hundred Carnations in different parts of the Borders. Heavenly evening. Reading. Writing."

Then, night falling, back inside within the glow of the candles they indulged so profligately. "Nine to One in the dressing room. Reading. A day of such Exquisite Such enjoyed retirement. So still. So silent."

So tightly controlled.

They seemed to experience liberation precisely because of the limitation of the System. This insistence on the ideal use of time was the point of their life together. The tourniquet of the System was a saving ligature.

No wonder I was impatient with Colette's wink-wink at what they were *really* up to, what couldn't be said in their age but could be named in her day (and even more in ours). Theirs was then and remains even more today the stranger passion, the one little understood—or even comprehended as passion.

Not erotic life, but the pleasure of the mind filling like the lower chamber of an hourglass with the slow-moving grains of a perfect day—sky, carnations, walking, reading, writing, Toasted Cheese, the presence of another who wishes to be so still, so silent too.

For a moment, don't dismiss it as trivial or creepy. For a moment, standing in the damp Bower (Spenser's bower of bliss? It comes to mind) it is possible to feel the fact of being alive as it breathes in, breathes out. It's a life. It's the life. It's the System. I suppose it's even love. For surely they loved each other. A love that passeth even the understanding of Eros.

All the people, the poets and princes, who preceded me to this distant place to visit—to pay homage, to claim connection to "the most Illustrious Virgins in Europe." How was it that the Ladies' strenuous "retirement" so quickly turned to society news? That their seclusion so soon translated into fame and fashion?

Their celebrity may have changed coloration over the decades, but their way of life remained essentially unaltered for fifty years. By the end (which came with Lady Eleanor's death, age ninety, in 1829, Sarah following her Beloved two years later in 1831), visitors to Llangollen did not always find the Ladies so enchanting, but simply very odd. The Scottish editor John Lockhart, visiting Plas Newydd in 1825 with his father-in-law, Sir Walter Scott, delighted in a malicious description of them wearing "enormous shoes, and men's hats, with their petticoats so tucked up, that at first glance of them fussing and tottering about . . . we took them for a couple of hazy or crazy old sailors."

Perhaps their earlier, more romantic celebrity, remarkable to us, was no great mystery in their own age. Their fame was a result or even the function of the deepest bond that first brought them together in the salons of their families ten years before their elopement to Wales, the bond that sustained their way of life for fifty years. Writing did it. Writing had inspired these two admirers of Rousseau, as had their taste for the novels and philosophy of the Enlightenment and refined French culture in the years preceding the Revolution.

Writing was the silver thread stitching together relations in their class, relations of love and especially of female friendship—from one bluestocking to another, from provincial whist-playing mother to urban-dwelling socialité daughter—Lady Betty Fownes in Kilkenny to her married daughter Sarah Tighe in Dublin. From the very epistolary Mrs. Thrale (onetime companion of Dr. Johnson) to the Ladies. And the busybody Harriet Bowdler—sister of the Shakespeare-purifying bowdlerizing Thomas Bowdler, editor of *The Family Shakespeare*). She too was a confidante of the Ladies, another of their letter writers, visitors, confabulators.

These women picked up a pen the way we tap on a cell phone, passing the latest to each other in reams of sinuous, dependent-clause-heavy prose, transcribing whole volleys of dialogue from dinners and tea parties, unfurling descriptions of spring blossoming and autumnal murk from long walks in all weathers. In a sense, they were all writing essays, meandering in their minds, and sometimes taking on questions of the day—slaveholding, environmental depredations (those satanic mills), the recent alarming rumors from France.

They were amateur Montaignes. But then, being an amateur was central to Montaigne's project, not its result but its core impulse. His *Essais,* his whatevers. The offhandedness and the intimacy of letters could also convey stray thoughts, arpeggios of feeling, formless forms. All this the Ladies and their correspondents adopted as essential to life.

But the analogy to the cell phone is wrong: the Ladies and

their friends weren't yakking, they were writing, sentences and paragraphs lending their expression, like Montaigne's, formality and the chance of longer shelf life through copying and quotation. And curiously, more revealing of self than conversation (because uninterrupted by social awareness).

Theirs was a writing world, a small sphere by the standards of our mass culture, moving not over media outlets but across the well-oiled tracks of correspondence, warmed and boiled over by heated gossip and rumor. In this closed but wordy culture of correspondence, "reputations could be made," according to Elizabeth Mavor, "without so much as publishing a book."

Letters were copied and shared, quoted, read aloud to visitors. And of course everyone was keeping a journal, annotating encounters with the eye not of an historian but a proto-novelist, keeping track, keeping score, assessing and attesting—and then quoting themselves from their journals back into their letters, a kind of self-publishing editorial project that kept these supposedly idle women very busy.

Writing—or passionate reading (which comes to the same thing in ardent bookish youth)—was the first attachment between Sarah and Eleanor when they met in their families' salons, Sarah a child of thirteen, Lady Eleanor, sharp-tongued, going nowhere in the marriage market, but suddenly on the way to becoming the soul mate to the shy, dependent orphan.

It was at first and for years before their elopement an epistolary friendship, words on the page allowing the two friends an intimacy that conversation could not equal, deepening attachment, confirming intimacy, heart to heart, mind to mind.

The letters flew between Woodstock and Butler Castle, great sheaves of shared feeling folded within the confines of envelopes ripped open and immediately responded to. Passionate paragraphs, the subject-verb-object of ardor. As Lady Betty said of Sarah after the elopement, expressing herself in her distracted but acute way, "Poor Soul if she had not been so fond of her pen so much would not have happened."

Nor are we entirely divorced from this writing romance. A priest told me recently that 40 percent of the weddings he performs now are, as he put it, Match.com marriages. These romances may start with a posted photograph, but no one gets beyond the picture without having to *write* a portrait to the other, for it turns out real self-disclosure still comes not from pictures but through words. And words on the page (or screen) are paradoxically more, not less, revealing than that first meet-for-coffee date. Even our way of describing it proves the point. We don't say, "Show me yourself." I want you in words, the narrative reveal: *Tell me about yourself. Tell me.*

Remember how strangely embarrassed he was, admitting he didn't like Skype when it first became possible on these research trips to call home for free—to *see* each other, to talk? *I miss the letters,* he said, almost sheepishly. Meaning the long email screeds I wrote every night and he replied to in the morning. *It's more intimate,* he said. *Brings you nearer.* Nearer even than the sight of the face, though of course we each kissed the screen, and laughed, touching the cold flat rectangle with our lips. *Write me, write me,* he said. Meaning, come nearer.

———

I return the orange umbrella to the woman at the teashop, who hopes I have enjoyed myself. We fall into conversation (another cup of tea), and she tells me with a shyness veering on quiet desperation (Thoreau comes to mind—another seeker after the perfect life system) that she used to work in nursing, but now that's over. There has been a sadness, a loss—she'd rather not say—but her life has . . . changed. I don't mention that my life has changed too. She is running the cash register at the teashop now. She has become devoted to the Ladies. She lives alone. Now. A loss. She repeats this word. *Such friends they were—Eleanor and Sarah.*

It must have been hard, she says, for Sarah after Eleanor . . . went. *Well, she only stayed on another two years.* Said thoughtfully, as if two years were doable.

This soft-edged woman probably my age, running the cash register—she's the one I've come all this way to meet, it occurs to me. Someone who understands them. Meditates on loss, weighs its heft. In considering the nature of the Ladies' attachment, their biographer calls theirs a "romantic friendship," saying this bond was "a once flourishing but now lost relationship." Romantic friendship may be extinct, but it does not go unmourned by the teashop cashier.

You'll put them in a book? she asks, wonder in her voice.

That's the plan, I say.

She nods—*They'll be hard to get.*

I walk back down the way I came, past the NO DOG FOUL-ING sign and the back gardens, down the steep hill into the little town. I won't be here much longer. Suddenly I realize—surely because of the sad woman in the teashop—that what I will remember most from this effort (it has been an effort to get here, even to be here, trying so strenuously to conjure a *lost relationship*) is the people who were supposed to not matter, not really, the extras of contemporary life.

The stars I have sought always exist in the past. But now—not so much. A shift of focus. The young waiter at the Corn Mill (*You're a nice lady, and you got here first, didn't you?*), Carol at the Cornerstone (*Glad to take in a stray, come anytime*), the grieving madonna at the tearoom cash register. I have taken more notes (*the ineluctable consequence of one's greatest inward energy*) on them, the supposed bit players, than on Plas Newydd, this place I went to such trouble to get myself to.

I stop at a flower shop—it's late, the store closing. I buy a handful of lilies, rather limp, all that's left in the metal bucket outside the door. The woman closing the shop takes the time to furl them in a sheet of paper printed with pale roses. With this wand of flowers I head to the churchyard where the three of them—Eleanor, Sarah, Mary Carryll—are buried.

The church is gray, stern and stony at the end of the long, grassy property, and of course not a Catholic church. Their System may have had a monastic tinge to it, but Sarah was ardently anti-Catholic. Part of the argument about "living and dying with Miss Butler" she made so passionately to her guardians concerned the Butler plan to dispatch troublesome Eleanor to a convent in France (what a fate that would have been on the eve of the Revolution). "I would do anything," she wrote to a friend in the midst of the upheaval before they were allowed to leave Ireland together, "to save Miss Butler from Popery and a Convent."

I have the churchyard to myself, and don't have to hunt around for the monument—for there it is, a triangular free-standing pediment of gray stone, each side devoted to one of them. Mary Carryll was the first to go, November 22, 1809. Her death was occasion for the monument's erection, to which the other two plaques would be added in due course.

A heavily end-rhymed poem (surely by Eleanor), honors the Ladies' faithful servant whose

> *Virtues dignified her humble birth*
> *And raised her mind above this sordid earth. . . .*
> *Reared by Two Friends who will her loss bemoan,*
> *Till with Her Ashes . . . Here shall rest, Their own.*

They were as good as their word. The plaque on the second side is "Sacred to the Memory of the Right Honorable Lady Eleanor Charlotte Butler," deceased June 2, 1829, aged ninety years, with every title and relationship to a title toted up ("Daughter of the Sixteenth, Sister of the Seventeenth Earls of Ormonde and Ossory, Aunt to the Late and to the Present Marquess of Ormonde"). Never mind that her Irish relatives would have nothing to do with her.

The list of her attributes, surely written by Sarah, include "Brilliant Vivacity of Mind," "Delight," "Excellence of Heart and . . . Manners worthy of Her Illustrious Birth," "amiable Condescension and Benevolence," and "various Perfections."

All these virtues, the plaque assures the reader, are, together with their possessor, now "enjoying their Eternal Reward, and by Her of whom for more than Fifty Years they constituted that Happiness Which . . . She trusts will be renewed When THIS TOMB Shall have closed Over Its Latest Tenant." A tongue-twisting form of bereavement from the grieving Sarah, a longing for death. That is, for reunion. Amazing—what would it be like to believe that? To see him again.

Sarah became that final Tenant two years later, December 9, 1831, age seventy-six. She must have composed the scant words on her own side of the pediment, unable to keep Eleanor entirely separate over on her side, giving her Beloved pride of place on her own plaque: "She did not long survive her beloved companion LADY ELEANOR BUTLER with whom she had lived in this valley for more than half a century of uninterrupted friendship—but they shall no more return to their House neither shall their place know them any more." As if they had eloped again, absconding yet deeper into their romantic retirement.

I wished I'd thought to get a flower to leave on the ground for all three of them. I considered taking one of the lilies I'd bought for Carol at the Cornerstone, but that would mean breaking the seal on the wrapping paper. I had nothing to leave as a token or salute, so I just stood, and then walked around the stone and its overwrought sentiment several times. My sneakers were damp from the wet grass, and there was nothing more to do here.

I went over to the Cornerstone before retrieving my roller bag at the Falls. Once again, when I knocked, Carol was there, opening the door in a flash, as if she had been waiting for me.

I wanted to thank her, I said, for taking me in yesterday. I handed over the bundle of wrapped lilies.

How kind, how good of you!

She unfurled the paper, and the lilies flopped out, withered, wilted. Obviously dead. They looked as if I'd rescued them from a trash bin.

We both looked at them for a lost moment. They were much worse than when I'd bought them—weren't they? They were like a patient who has been ailing but is not expected to die, and then just gives up the ghost when the family turns away for a moment.

I was mortified. They'd been fresh an hour before, I heard myself muttering. I didn't know what had happened. And so on, twisting in the wind there on the Cornerstone doorstep.

Carol looked at the lilies with an indulgent, even fond expression, and then up at me with an entirely accepting face, and said, *Well, but it's always the thought that counts, isn't it? That's what I say, it's the thought counts.*

Friend was the word the Ladies insisted on, the relation they claimed from the start to the end of their long life together. Not "lover," or "spouse," not "mate," certainly not "partner," though they referred to each other in their journals, even in letters to friends, as *my Beloved,* so frequent a term that Sarah often shortened it to "my B." The word in their time and place had the breezy social affection of our "darling," fond but casual. It was the endearment Dorothy and William Wordsworth, also living the cottage life of retirement and poetry in the Lake District at that time, used for one another.

The Ladies' *romantic friendship,* that "once flourishing but now lost relationship." Strange to think of a form of love going extinct, like a carrier pigeon, a rare tortoise, a lilac or apple whose seeds are not to be found anymore, the scent and taste of the thing long lost, never to be touched again. An extinct relationship.

The reason for this "loss," of course, is that it is almost impossible for the contemporary mind to read a passion like theirs (*my Beloved!*) as anything but erotic, and therefore homoerotic. They were lesbians—good for them, we say. What their biographer calls lost, most modern, self-congratulating "liberated" minds (heterosexual or otherwise) see as more fully found. They were out, we say. And then think we understand, as Colette assumed she did, even if they didn't themselves, what they were up to.

They were aware of the possibility. They were appalled by the notion. Even more, they cared about the life they had so carefully chosen and crafted, the meaning they had given to living a retired life. The System. But before long they were treated to gossip—they were lovers, their elopement the result of an *unnatural* passion. In July 1791, three years after their settling in Llangollen, an article in the *General Evening Post* so offended the Ladies that Eleanor immediately wrote to cancel their subscription "for Essential reasons."

One reason really: under the headline "Extraordinary Female Affection," the unsigned reporter described in broad if sometimes inaccurate detail the story of their flight from Ireland and their life together as "the Ladies of a certain Welsh Vale." The implication was clear: they were Sapphists.

The Ladies sought out no less a friend than Edmund Burke for redress to this grievance against their life, their System, and the nature of the love they practiced.

Burke took up their cause, saying he too had responded to the article "with the indignation felt by every worthy mind." What would he have said, I wondered, jumping centuries again, to Colette's grease-monkey Eleanor and the amputated breasts?

In the event, he was the soul of gallantry. But he had to advise them, as prudent lawyers often must, that filing suit for libel was a game hardly worth the candle. "Your consolation," he said, "must be that you suffer only by the baseness of the age you live in."

They were suffering for their "virtues," he reminded them, qualities that earned them the highest regard among those who "esteem honour, friendship, principle, and dignity of thinking."

Let it go, as people say in our own *whatever* age.

And, amazingly, given the high horse Lady Eleanor so often rode, they did just that. They let it go. In the next day's journal, as if no feather had been ruffled, no insult absorbed, Eleanor was able to report (as she routinely did, day by day, year after year, summing up the preceding twenty-four hours) that she and Sarah had once again gloried in "a day of delightful retirement."

In the unrivaled world of private life and in the journal,

that book whose publication is confined to heart and hearth, there is no higher court. Life lived, life described, the bits and pieces of the day collected, vignette by vignette. And thus, life affirmed. More than enough.

Send the visitors off to the Hand, light the candles in the dressing room, curl up for a bit of Rousseau, Mary Carryll having made up the fire, all so snug. The System is the thing as, arm in arm, the two of them walk the Home Circuit, pausing to consider the placement of the carnations, the question of an addition to the Shrubbery, the utter impossibility that fifty years have passed—already!—in the succession of these *Celestial glorious* days, these *heavenly* evenings.

Winter now, back in St. Paul, the Ladies tucked away in my notebooks as they were cold nights in their dressing room, curtains drawn, the fire glowing—their fire in the eighteenth century, mine here in the twenty-first.

I'm still reading Montaigne. I seem to feel I have to *prepare* to visit his tower—I can't just show up in Bordeaux as I did in Llangollen. Bulk up on the *Essais,* marginal notes in the Donald M. Frame biography. More notes on the recent books by other people writing about Montaigne.

One of the oddities—or inevitabilities—of the reading life is that, like every aspect of human habit (food, clothes, design), it has its fashions. During the latter-day American belle epoque, the era of our prideful assurance over having "won the Cold War," the self-regarding age when Donald Trump's "little hands" began shellacking so much real estate with gold—it seemed everyone was reading (or intending to read) Proust. I was—intending to. Books about reading Proust became popular in the 1980s and 1990s—*How Proust Can Save Your Life, The Year of Reading Proust.* The jeweled canvas of the earlier belle epoque was the mirror of our own garish surface. One world winking at another.

This period of Proustaphilia coincided with our own *entre deux guerres.* How shockingly brief that Pax Americana was—from the fall of the Berlin Wall in October 1989 to the fall of the Twin Towers in September 2001. We had the heady illusion of winning, being on top, running the show. The end of history? That idea floated around for a while in the absurd arrogance of the age.

The end of history came to its own shattering end, of course. The pause between the world wars (1918 to 1939) when Proust's masterpiece was composed and published was a period considerably longer than our own age of glee or indifference (or was it just self-indulgence?)—their twenty-one years to our twelve. Whether it was 9/11 or, later, the economic meltdown and recession, suddenly (it seemed sudden), with the crash of our illusions, stylish readers were swapping out Proust for Montaigne, and books about reading the *Essais* began to take the place of those about reading *In Search of Lost Time.*

Why Montaigne? Why now? I asked you that when I started all this. You were still here to ask, across the yellow kitchen table. Not that you believed in answering such questions.

That's why you're writing this—to find out.

You were the real reader, pitch-perfect ear, cunning combination of humility and boldness, responding to the page before you. Starkly independent mind. A gallant reader, I'd say now. Leaving clippings on my desk, sending me links on email. Pursuing any question or curiosity I mentioned at the yellow kitchen table. My research fellow. Your Post-it note on the clipping from the twenty-fifth anniversary of the Velvet Revolution in Prague: *Drst: What about how leisure might fit in with the Cold War? A connection? Discuss!*

Maybe Montaigne appeals to this age because he "retired"— that word again. You thought I might have a point there. He had left the world of power and command, sequestered himself in his tower to investigate the furnishings of his mind. Individual consciousness was his subject, not the sweep of his tumultuous era. Yet his was an age of terror and cruelty, crying out for explanation, for a big-picture narrative of its seismic divisions. Whereas Proust's world floated on the airless steadiness of the cork-lined room where in shadow he spun his vast magnificence.

In times of peace the age itself is the story, leisurely with intrigue, gossip, affairs of state, affairs of love—busy, busy, busy with its social self, making massive formal shapes. In times of terror like Montaigne's, like ours, we (we readers) seek instead the sane singular voice, alone with its thoughts, maybe to assure ourselves that sanity does exist somewhere, and the self, the littleness of personhood is somewhere alive, taking its notes. And that this matters. We know the awful part, the sweep of history's cruelties. We want the singular voice, abiding. This is why a little girl keeping a diary in an Amsterdam attic is "the voice of the Holocaust."

Details, tossed into the shoebox of the mind, fragments.

Not a regal "story" riding its narrative arc. Just a bunch of snapshots, never amounting to a shape, but too tender to be tossed.

Something like that, darling?

In this age of terror and the terror *of* terror, I've joined the ranks of those reading Montaigne, the sane man in his insane world. A man alone in a room with words, not sorting out his "world." Sorting his mind.

My reading isn't scholarship—just picking up a scent in the air, following it. An attempt to find, across the maw of our distant centuries, some kind of explanation for the kinship I feel. Not just kinship. Some kind of help. Call it solace.

Montaigne was a reader himself, that's one thing. His *Essais* are studded with quotations—especially when he first started his project. He intended to follow the Stoic model, *doing philosophy to learn how to die*. Over the kitchen table, you said that was when he was just fooling around, showing off, trying to be a writer. That was when he was something of a pedant. You can't *learn* to die, you said. You just die.

Tough reader you always were.

So what's the difference between writing the big picture (Proust) and collecting small takes (Montaigne)? A question we batted back and forth across the yellow kitchen table, the coffee getting cold. The novel is committed to design. On this we agreed, you with your reverence for Joyce's *Ulysses* (your annual Bloomsday party, everyone invited to read a passage), me with my impatience over his fussiness, my claims for Fitzgerald. *Fitzgerald! You're comparing Fitzgerald to Joyce?* We let that one lie on the table.

Oh yes, we fought, and not just over literature. But we could never seem, afterward, to remember what our furies were about. You would walk out of the room. I would hector— *Come back here! You coward!* I fretted over our fights—I wanted a "perfect relationship." *No!* you said. *Fights are good! They let you have these sweet reconciliations.*

Even a short novel has a trajectory—my point, and why you *can* compare *Gatsby* to *Ulysses.*

Do you always have to get the last word?

What I was trying to explain: the final page of any novel is a destination, the creation of form offering the illusion of inevitability, the denial of chaos. We don't love novels because they are like life, but because they are unlike it—deftly organized, filled with the satisfaction of shape. This shapeliness isn't "closure," a modern comfort word too airlessly psychological for the deep gratifications storytelling provides. The great carapace of the novel puts a bridle on the stampede of detail.

And yet the great unsorted pile of detail—that's what a life is. Not the organization of details into shape (that's the novel), but the recognition of the welter of life—notetaking, James's *ineluctable consequence of one's greatest inward energy . . . to take them . . . as natural as to look, to think, to feel, to recognize, to remember.*

You understood—I think you did—that I didn't think of notetaking as *material*, bricks for the great architecture of a book, even if Henry James did. I was taking them for themselves. Life is not a *story,* a settled version. It's an unsorted heap of images we keep going through, the familiar snaps taken up and regarded, then tossed back until, unbidden, they rise again, images that float to the surface of the mind, rise, fall, drift—and return only to drift away again in shadow. They never quite die, and they never achieve form. They are the makings of a life, not of a narrative. Not art, but life trailing its poignant desire for art. Call them vignettes, these things we finger and drop again into their shoebox.

We all have these snippets rolling around, not stories we tell, just photos that refuse to fade entirely away. These are the framed moments that decide a life and are lost to art because they aren't complete, have no resolution. They're nothing much. *Essais, vignettes, memoirs*—the French words our stalwart form-seeking Anglophone mind must borrow to articulate our formlessness.

Deep winter as I sit here in our drafty old St. Paul house, the lunar white surface of the deepest season inviting vignettes into the mind, the ice-cold of memory. These memory shards can even predate us. My earliest is more legacy than memory: Uncle Frankie, my father's older brother, adored hero son of the Czech granny, a blacksmith (such an antique profession), making his way as a semipro welterweight prizefighter. Frankie of the dashing good looks, the idealism, promising his twin sister Lillian (my favorite aunt) a diamond ring if she would stay in high school and graduate while he—this is the Depression—gets a job. Frankie, killed in that terrible industrial accident in 1936. He'd been given a pickup job at Schmidt Brewery (he'd lost his railroad job in the lay-offs of the Depression) and was repairing a valve when some-one (who?) turned on the boiling water, and it gushed in, sweeping him into the scalding whirlwind. He survived three weeks, conscious, knowing it was the end.

I've put him in every book I've written, managed to wedge him in somehow or other, the lost hero, the good guy I never met. Did I make it up or is it true that he somehow grabbed hold of the ladder up and out of the giant copper vat, but slipped and splashed fatally back into the cauldron? I see it—I've always seen it. It was part of being in our family. I was given to believe that "after the War" he would have been saved because of all the burn treatments developed then. So war was good in its way. *We had to drop the bomb, darling. It saved lives.*

Frankie was gone—and therefore (even as a child it felt like "therefore") he was more present than anyone. The terri-ble, decisive accident. "I lost that diamond ring," Aunt Lillian said. "I lost it." And you knew what she meant. The ring of relationship gone. From book to book there always seemed to be a little something left over I had not described, so I pulled him in again with the new detail. The diamond ring, for ex-ample: I've never mentioned that till now. Maybe I'd forgotten it. But there it always was, and with it my aunt's face, not just sad but remorseful, as if losing the ring had been part of the accident.

A man called me after my first book was published, some-one from the old Czech neighborhood. He had known Frankie, worked with him. He wanted to meet me, talk to me. "I read your book," he said, giving the sense that this had taken considerable effort. We met in an old art deco bar, one now gentrified, but then, in the 1980s, fading into itself from the era he and Frankie had shared as young men.

I want to tell you something, he said.

He fussed around, ordered a beer, showed me some newspaper clippings—I can't remember what they were about. I was—God help me—bored. He was old, of course, something of a gasbag. I wasn't sure he had actually read my book after all. He said "all of West Seventh" (the main street of the Czech neighborhood by the brewery where my family lived, where I'd been born) was lined four deep from Schmidt's to St. Stan's where the funeral was. Men with their hats off, women weeping. Crying right there on the street.

Another detail I've never mentioned until now—the crowds on the street, mourning the workingman hero, the handsome prizefighter.

That was what he wanted to tell me, I figured—give me that sense of importance. I thanked him, and though I saw that he would like to sit longer in the smoky room, I wanted to go. And I did. On to the next thing.

Surely he's long gone by now, the old man stuffing his clippings into his coat pocket, ordering another beer, staying in the dim bar after I scurried away, glad to be free of him.

Then last year he appeared again—not him, but the rest of his message. I think that's what appeared. Another boring event, another just-say-no occasion where I had shown up, done what was asked of me. You can count on me, and there I was at the Czech hall where my grandparents had danced. I was supposed to read an excerpt about the old neighborhood from my first book, one I never read from anymore, the one the old man had wanted to talk about. The program, devoted to "the working-class history of St. Paul," was organized by the state historical society. Six people engaged in family history projects were making presentations, one after another, unused to public speaking, yammering away. Yet another way to lose an evening of life, sitting there, listening, pretending to listen, making to-do lists in my head.

I was second to last on the program, read my couple of pages, sat down, waiting for it to be over—just one more person to go, an older woman with a bad hip shagging up to the front to report on her father, a blacksmith many years dead. She displayed a photograph, a long horizontal print crowded with workingmen outside the old Great Northern Railway shops. The names of the men were on the back, she said, and she began reading them off. Good Lord—this is never going to end, tears of boredom forming in the corners of my eyes. *Frank Hampl,* she read, the name leaping out of her litany like a reprimand.

I went up to her afterward, asked to see the photo, knowing I couldn't possibly pick him out of the group. My eye went right to him, the family laser beam latching. He looked tough and romantic, a young Johnny Depp. A tender bruiser. Hollywood in that face, one of those fuck-you-love-me faces of the bad-boy lead. *You know,* the woman said shyly, *they say it wasn't an accident.*

I stared at her. The hideous fall into the boiling vat of water, the poor guy (as my father always added) who hadn't realized Frankie was down there—he had to live with that. The accident.

He was very prominent in the union, you know, this daughter of a brother blacksmith was saying as we both stared at the historical photo. *Very big in the union effort. Some thought it wasn't no accident.*

The dim deco bar, the man cramming old clippings in his jacket pocket. *I have something I want to tell you.*

If I had stayed for his story, instead of just tossing the vignette in the beaten-up shoebox of memory . . . well, we'll never know now, will we? Was he in possession of *this* vignette, the telling moment? Or was he—was it possible— was he . . . the *poor guy?* Live with it, live with never knowing. Plenty to ponder, nothing, finally, to narrate. This is life, not art.

The welter of images, the absence of a controlling narrative. Life itself in its disarray, being life, refusing to be tidied into a story. And then the story refusing to be refused. Protesting formlessness. Insisting on resolution, on shape.

I'll never write about Frankie again. He isn't a vignette anymore. And never again can it be an accident.

Now, warm in our winter house, another vignette comes flickering forward as the light fades tonight—one I never told you, which is strange, given the subject, given that I told you everything, sometimes over and over again (*crazy about you, just crazy about you*). This one is mine and not an inheritance:

Midwinter, a Saturday afternoon at the Olympic, the skating rink across the street from the house where I grew up. The day is gray. A piercing cold safeguards the freshly flooded ice, keeps it hard. We skate on the cloudy glass, barely nicked by the early skaters, of which, as always, I am one. This is years before the heart-thumping Friday nights when I will hyperventilate over whether Tommy Hough or Billy McGehan or *someone* will ask me to skate with him. My arctic entry into erotic life is years ahead, but it will always have something of ice in it.

This is still childhood. We're skating separately, boys zigzagging on their blunt hockey skates, practicing slap shots with their sticks, girls treading along in white boots whose slim blades have toe picks that look as if the metal were cut with pinking shears. We skate, five girls in a row, holding hands. What will we do when we grow up? This is our subject.

We glide round and round. Carol Bardis says, "I'm going to have five children, same as my mom." Joyce O'Neill is quick with her own showy number: "Ten," she says tartly, at nine already a Catholic matron who will take her chances with the rhythm method.

I'm a crack skater, an accomplishment I wear with feigned modesty. I'm on the ice every day, practicing relentlessly. I would like skating lessons, but my father says no, I will stick with the piano. We can only afford one extra. I can pull myself into a tight column, spinning like a wand without falling in a dizzy heap. Cutting the ice backward, pivoting forward, fearless in my turns and jumps, executing swan dives and the rarely attempted shoot-the-duck that involves a crouch, speeding on one skate—all this I do. Even backwards I do this.

Other skaters stop and watch me. Sometimes they cheer. I pretend not to notice, pretend to be skating just for the pleasure of it. And it is a pleasure, though also it is this other thing. My cold little star glows inwardly, all faces turned toward me. But right now I'm just skating like everybody else, round and round the perfect ice with my friends as they announce their futures. I'm on the outside, taking broader strides than anyone else in the line as we round the curve near the warming house.

Katy Masters will enter the convent, she says gravely, trumping everyone and bringing things to a momentary silence. Eileen McPherson, a sensible girl, soldiers on: she has decided on two, a boy (first) and a girl. She speaks with satisfaction as of something nicely settled.

My turn. They're waiting for me, the big talker, to ante up. What is my number? Always vying for first place, will I join Katy Masters in the convent?

Confusion seizes me. Panic flutters in a zigzag neural pattern from brain to stomach and back again. An inner fizz of distress spreads everywhere. This is mixed up with something else I can't locate though it's even worse. Much later I recognize this other thing as shame, an emotion unfamiliar to me in my easy glory as a beloved child with good-girl bona fides, boring Father Kennedy and even myself with a tedious grocery list of low-grade repetitive sins toted up for confession on Saturday nights.

I drop Eileen's hand, fending off suffocation, and peel

away in a showy flourish. No one thinks this odd—we form brief skating lines, and then sail off alone or go to the warming house for hot chocolate. The ice is free space. And everyone knows I like to skate fast, off on my own.

But what is this, what's happening? Why must I run away from this cheerful game? Why can't I sing out how many children will be mine in the gauzy phantasm of the future we love to inhabit?

I know why. Also I don't know. That is, I know what it *is,* but I'm baffled by *why* it is.

Zero. That's my number. That's how many children I will have. This is not a wish, not a decision. It's not even a bravura abdication of the sort Katy Masters has announced. It is a recognition. This seed of self, unitary and vacant, is dead center, the moon-colored essence of my fate. It has announced itself at this icy moment and without my permission: age ten, winter all around me, and zero is my number. Why is that my number? I don't know. But it is.

I skate away, take to the ice. I shoot the duck, I rise again and lift my outstretched leg in a perfectly executed swan dive, winging my arms out, my head up to the blank sky. I do my tricks.

I don't understand what has happened. But that it *has* happened—that I know. It is a framed moment, not a story, but something much smaller, a spark of meaning I will return to all my life. The DNA of identity. What, much later, I learn is a vignette, a photo frayed at the edges, its old silver frame stowed in the dark attic of the mind.

A bare fragment of story, caught in the sticky amber of

recollection. It isn't even a subject, it's the threshold of a subject, a necessary opening to a wider interior to be explored, considered, read like the book it wants to become. It is something insubstantial made substantial sheerly by virtue of its indelibility. A vignette shifts the mind away from storytelling into speculation. Why, why? A bit of narrative sand irritating itself into a pearl of thought. An *essai* in the making.

The vignette is the construction site for a palace of values, a hand-built habitation, well sited, with views and loggias, stately gathering rooms and odd, intimate nooks. It leads down the rabbit hole of thought, not to the taut wire of narrative. And this, on the smooth surface of our home ice, is my first.

But is it art?

It is not. It's life. That's all, the sand-grit that works its way under the shell of the self. There are so many shifting sands, glinting in the winter light, moments that make a life, though not, alas, a story.

Summer now, and I'm sitting at Vlasta's table, the Formica rectangle wedged between the tiny dark kitchen and the window along a scant passageway, another alleged room in this jigsaw apartment. A heavy drape with a jungle design hangs on a rod and serves as a door to the bath just behind my chair. Nothing is wasted here, every inch has a purpose, brought smartly forward for its moment, then falling back in formation until called up again. For now, this corridor serves as dining room.

When Vlasta doesn't have us out walking or hiking in the wine country of south Moravia, this is where I am every late July—at her table, taking in her perfect meals as if they too were a trek we embark on, hour after hour, moving slowly in place over the cuisine of the region she commands as surely as she knows the land, the vineyards, the forest trails. Restaurants are out of the question—foolishly expensive and *that* food. No, no, no. Put that credit card away!

It won't be long before the flower-patterned platters start emerging from the closet-kitchen. For now I'm supposed to keep sipping Becherovka from one of her mother's Moser liqueur glasses, the cut glass incised so sharply it seems it would nick your finger if you didn't handle it carefully. But you—that is, I—want to do everything carefully, gently here. It's the point of being at her table. Rush has left the room, food has slowed the pulse. Pavarotti comes forward again— *One of the very nicest things about life is the way we must regularly stop whatever it is we are doing and devote our attention to eating.*

Gauze curtains over the window barely obscure, outside, ranks of the same kind of building we're in—what the Czechs call *panalaky,* panel buildings, dour construction dating from the socialist era, slabs of cheaply made high-rises for workers to live in, or be warehoused.

To be fair, these apartment complexes in Znojmo, a provincial south Moravian capital near the Austrian border, are less dismal than the taller high-rises of the Minneapolis West Bank where recently arrived Somalis now make their homes, turning that early-twentieth-century Scandinavian immigrant enclave of cottages and kitchen gardens into a neighborhood of halal markets.

Modernism for the masses is aging in place everywhere, its proud reach now a bleak supplication to high heaven. A hopeful, if arrogant architecture. Its ideal lives on in its ragged reality—rising, yet sagging somehow, on both sides of what was for so long the essential opposition of my lifetime: East/West.

Znojmo's *panalaky* offer more cheer now than the aging Minneapolis high-rises—the cheap windows here have been replaced with triple-glazed insets, the elevators are sleek and assured. These buildings, once the gloom gray of the socialist color wheel (brown, gray, tarnish black), have been rouged up and wink in ice-cream pastels. Vlasta's building is banana yellow. She owns her own apartment—private ownership is back, whereas the Minneapolis buildings are public housing rentals, a reversal of Cold War economic patterns.

I've been returning these recent summers to Vlasta's apartment, driving from Prague to Znojmo with my friend and hers Anna, a cardiologist and public health doctor I met in Prague right after the end of the Cold War. The two of them are hiking buddies, mad trekkers, mushroom hunters, knowers of forest lore, hardy campers, both aging out of the endurance hikes that brought them together years ago, but still game. I often have to stop on our hikes, pretending I'm taking in the view while they soldier on. In fact, I'm gasping to catch my breath.

I know why I return, not for one of my "subjects," though this year I plan to seek out another of my monastic heroes— not *you and your nuns* this time, but me and my monk: Gregor Mendel. *The pea plant man?* you said, puzzled, when I first proposed him as one of my exemplars of leisure. *Why not Linnaeus?* you said. If I was thinking about a life given over to the pacific naming and ordering of the flora world, the innocent age of science, wouldn't Linnaeus be my man? After all, as I'd told you, my florist father thought of naming me Linnaea.

But no—I'll get to that, darling. Remember your Post-it note attached to the clipping about the twenty-fifth anniversary of Prague's Velvet Revolution? *What about how leisure fits in with the Cold War? Didn't you say something about that at dinner? A connection? Discuss!*

You're the one who googled, on a hunch, the date of Churchill's Iron Curtain speech in Fulton, Missouri—March 5, 1946. *Seven days before you were born!* How pleased you were with that bit of research, making world history part of my lifeline.

But beyond Gregor Mendel, what I'm looking for is right here at this small table, the Moser liqueur glass fracturing light onto the embroidered place mat (the meticulous work of Vlasta's long-dead mother), the linen starched, ironed solid as plywood, yellow thread flowers with their green vine as perfect on the reverse as on the front. Care and tending, the art of domesticity—the art of gardening too, Gregor Mendel's art. The force field of private life facing off against history's hammer (and sickle). Vlasta and Anna have lived their lives—except this coda we're in now—on the colder side of the Cold War. Yet here, I keep finding, is warmth curiously missing in America after all.

The meal will be served in courses by pixie-like Vlasta, never-married Vlasta, who cared for her father and mother until they finally left the planet in their nineties. She's well into her seventies, small pert head, precise movements, an operating room nurse's sense of order, though in fact she worked as a shop assistant in a state-owned hardware store. She lives now on a pension no American graduate student could imagine surviving on. Even Anna, who was not favored under Communism and has not thrived under the new market economy, shakes her head in wonder: how does Vlasta manage?

Light on her feet, quick, exact. An artist of the day, snapping her perfectly laundered linens on our guest cots, practically saluting from her high command on the battlement of the beautiful meal. Reed thin, an Ariel of the dumpling, sprite of a melting pork roast, beef *svíčková* limpid in its cream and tart berry sauce. And much to be said about the astonishing reincarnations she resurrects from cabbage, and pastries so airy they seem about to levitate off the faded china platter. This is the food of my Czech grandmother who left this region at the end of the nineteenth century and became a cook for "the rich" in St. Paul. Same food, same deft touch, same tricksy spirit. Paradoxically, the same ability to purvey luxury out of poverty.

Leisure, we tend to think, belongs to wealth. Its ease is a result or symptom of success, a sign of an excess of riches. It's what you get when you've clawed your way—or your father or grandfather did—to the top. Didn't the Romans with their *otium cum dignitate* require a slave class to do the heavy lifting to assure their life under the grape arbors? Hasn't history always relied on the toil of designated classes or castes to let it *be* a civilization? The shame of it—the cost of leisure being someone else's hard labor and broken body. My grandmother's bowed legs—*rickets,* my father said, frowning, when I asked about her cartoonish stance.

My grandmother must have sensed the latent shame of

"the nobles," as she called the people she first served as a girl in Europe. Later in America, still a girl, becoming a culinary wizard who cooked for the "rich," the word she used—as we did—to indicate her employers with amused, even affectionate contempt. We always had the sense, around her table, that we were having more fun. Being us was better than being them. There was something slightly ridiculous about being rich. In a college sociology course we were asked to name our socioeconomic class—working class, middle class, upper middle class, wealth (which had just that one word, "wealth" apparently lifted above class categories, in a range of its own). These were the choices. I was stumped. Finally I wrote—I still think accurately—*serving class.*

After her, the next generation of women, her daughters, my aunts, childless stay-at-home wives who cooked for their uxorious husbands, whose lunch pails they outfitted with snugly wrapped sandwiches, scratch-baked slices of cake, a thermos of coffee. My Irish mother, "a working woman" (her proud term for her file clerk job), who married into this food-obsessed clan, was aghast at all this effort. She was glad, she said, to be "born in the frozen food age."

I first came to Czechoslovakia (as it was then), during the Cold War, because of this Czech grandmother (the iconic Czech novel is *Babička*—*Granny*—the domestic goddess of the nineteenth-century Czech Romantic movement, a touchstone not simply of family, but of the nation, the familiar grandmother figure as a stealth political operative with her *knedlíky* and *kolačky*). But even if my own Czech granny was part of my urgency in getting here, oddly enough, I didn't seek out her past once I arrived. It was not she, after all, who first brought me here, but an unexpected collision with history.

Get me the World!

August 20, 1968, just past 11 p.m. Eddie Hadro, city editor of the *St. Paul Pioneer Press,* is jabbing his pencil in my direction. He does this every night about this time, the pencil a dart he's aiming from his outstretched arm.

The newsroom is straight out of *Front Page,* bottles of rye stowed in reporters' desk drawers, an old-timer with a cigarette drooping stereotypically from his lip, writing up the police blotter. Ash falls on his faux silk tie as he rolls a sheet of grainy copy paper over the platen of his Royal. Head cocked, snugging the telephone receiver to his shoulder, he's growling, "Yeah, yeah, I got that, but spell the last name—some Polack."

The rat-a-tat-tat of dusty typewriters, furious swearing when a key sticks, though only the sportswriters in the back by the morgue say *fuck,* pronounced in lowered, sacramental tones. They mutter an apology if a girl (not yet a *woman*) is passing by. But everybody, girls and men alike, curses with relish in the newsroom as nobody, then, swore in public. *Damn, shit, hell no, bet your ass.* In the night newsroom, the practitioners of journalism sliced into the guts of language as sure as surgeons opening up the hidden parts of the body. We talked dirty; it was a professional thing.

My first job out of college. A job I almost didn't get because working the night desk meant that at the end of the shift, like everybody else sitting around the horseshoe desk writing headlines and editing copy, I would have to walk in the dark to my car (loaned by my mother who worked days as a file clerk at a college library). A girl walking alone, downtown, past 2 a.m.? Reason to be passed over. I was given the job finally because several of the men on the desk, middle-aged with children close to my age, had said sure, they'd walk the girl to her car. *Will someone be waiting up for you at home?* the managing editor asked me. How it was in 1968 in St. Paul.

And how I came to be charged with *The News of the World,* a boxed quarter page, above the fold inside page one, over the ads. This tidy box, edited from UPI or AP wire dispatches, usually took care of most matters beyond St. Paul. Eddie Hadro signaled with his pencil around 11 p.m., before the copy boy came back with the damp sandwiches from Di-Gidio's, and off I trotted, a well-trained retriever. Like a small-time bookie, Eddie Hadro actually wore a green visor and black sleeve protectors he peeled off at the end of the night. "Actually" because it all seems unreal now, the way the past does when it comes back in the sureness of its abandoned details.

I walked over to the glassed-in room behind us that housed the UPI and AP teletypes. Were these two gray metal machines in this sequestered space, behind a glass door, because they made a lot of noise? Or because they were, in spite of their bulk, terribly delicate mechanisms that required a sterile ICU? It wasn't clear. But entering the room was a step away from St. Paul, away from the littleness of our concerns, a tiptoe into the vast workings of the World.

Inside this isolation booth there was no swearing, no furious X-ing out of copy, no yellow copy paper reeled onto pitted platens, no impatient slam of carriage returns. Just the relentless stamping out of disembodied sentences in a rote rhythm unlike real writing. This auto-dictation emanated from a disembodied correspondent way out there somewhere—the World itself sending its implacable communiqués from its Olympian remove.

Sometimes the world did overtake St. Paul and claimed the front page. A lot had happened in the six months I'd been working at the paper. LBJ had announced he would not run again for president—we had to remake the front page that night. Martin Luther King was murdered, but that happened before Eddie Hadro had made up page one, so doing the banner headline posed no problem. Then, in June, another hard knock from the world—Bobby Kennedy in California was shot. Given the two-hour time difference, past deadline (so to speak)—another front page to be reset. A deep rivalist pleasure: the *Minneapolis Tribune* didn't get the story in time.

But this late August night was quiet, the world apparently on vacation. *Europe is asleep,* I sometimes thought with a kind of awe as I opened the glass door to the machines. Except for Vietnam where we had no business, to me "the World" was Europe. I spent my days off "clean for Gene," campaigning for Eugene McCarthy. Of course I was against the war, and hated Hubert Humphrey, to my parents' dismay—how could I be against Hubert? He'd beat the Dixiecrats.

I closed the door behind me and approached the UPI machine, positioned against the back wall, silent and broody in its glass room. How long did I stand there? It could not have been long, but a spacious caesura of time as I waited before the bulky machine, looking through the cloudy glass over the roll of gray paper, poised for it to say something.

And then it spoke, a Ouija board spelling out its occult message. To me, alone, locked in our séance:

PRAGUE, Aug. 21, 1968 (UPI)—*Invasion forces from Russia and its satellites occupied Czechoslovakia with troops, tanks and jet planes against sporadic resistance today and snuffed out the country's experiment in liberal reform.—Street fighting in Prague left some dead and wounded as thousands of Czechoslovaks surged into the streets and shouted defiance of the invaders.*

Cannon, machine-gun and small arms fire crashed and rattled through the night in the capital and in Bratislava, where two weeks ago the Russians agreed to let Czechoslovakia have its liberal regime.

Except I wasn't reading the dispatch in these complete sentences and paragraphs. The machine had a peculiar tic, clearing its mechanical throat before speaking. It whirred and clicked in place for a moment, as if deliberating how to say what it had to say. Then the letters began to jerk in staccato onto the soft gray paper, pausing now and again, and jolting forward again. Standing there, I had the sensation not of reading a written report, but of watching it being composed before my widening eyes from a great, impenetrable distance.

The first word—the dateline Prague—startled me even before the rest came tapping out. Prague, where my family had come from, my grandmother, the Czech peasant, whose letters in English I began ghostwriting in grade school as soon as I commanded cursive. My first freelance job.

Prague, I understood, was not part of the World. It was out of the running as a location. We called it, as my grandmother did, the old country, a former place. Anyway, it was unreachable. Prague was *behind the Iron Curtain,* a metaphor so profound it was not a figure of speech, but a feature of landscape more real than the forests and mountains that divided Bohemia from West Germany, Moravia from Austria.

News of Dubček and the Prague Spring had penetrated this iron impasse, and it seemed there was going to be something called "socialism with a human face." But on this August night, standing alone as the invasion of Czechoslovakia jittered onto the gray paper, what mattered was that I knew something of the world—the World—that no one else in St. Paul, not even Eddie Hadro, knew.

I tore the sheet from the machine, walked out of the glass room to the city desk, past the slot man in charge of the copy desk. I held out the UPI dispatch to Eddie Hadro. As he reached for it I said, "We're going to have to remake page one." This in a voice of authority I had never before possessed in the newsroom or anywhere else for that matter.

I had Eddie Hadro's full attention, another first. "The Russians have invaded Prague," I said neutrally, a woman privy to the secret movement of troops and the intentions of empire, standing tall before this local working stiff in his green visor, as I offloaded intel from my position behind enemy lines. In my hand I held the World.

Was that the moment that decided I must go there—behind the Iron Curtain? It wasn't really a decision, more a response to a call. *Listen to your inner voice, children. It will guide you.* That stern invitation to follow the directives of the inner self is the deepest, most enduring aspect of a Catholic childhood. The sovereignty of it, the command given over to the still un-formed child. The power of it. It's a more decisive legacy than the much invoked "Catholic guilt" I'm often told I suffer from as from a congenital illness, a judgment offered with amused certainty by almost complete strangers.

It took some years after that August night to get there, to follow the *inner voice*—graduate school (poetry instead of journalism, another inner voice directive), then back working in journalism again. But in 1975, I quit a good editing job (everyone said) at the local public radio station. With a ma-rine blue backpack meant for tenting in the Boundary Waters humped on my back and the cheapest transatlantic ticket I could find—Winnipeg to London, and then by "boat train," as the old novels put it, to the Continent—I finally reached Cheb, the Czech border town featuring a rickety Cold War guard tower right out of an early Le Carré novel.

I was behind the Iron Curtain. I had never been "any-where" before (Canada didn't count). I thought—I told people—I was going to Czechoslovakia to "find my roots." I was fascinated—or dogged—by what I thought of as "the lin-gering life of immigration," the idea that just because my family had left Europe, they weren't entirely in or of America.

Maybe I wasn't either—this in spite of the fact that I didn't speak Czech, and American English was not only my native language, but my métier. I considered myself a writer. I was pretty much alone in this belief, but I didn't care. I didn't trust anyone over thirty—I trusted my inner voice. I was making my way. *Hot damn,* as the guys on the night desk would say.

Some burr of "the old world" had stuck to me as I walked through my family life. The immigrants themselves were dying off—grandmothers, grandfathers of the Great Immigration spanning the nineteenth and early twentieth centuries—taking with them their languages and foreign, fading memories, leaving behind a few recipes and stray words (at home we called beer *pivo,* and potatoes were *brambory*).

Alex Haley's *Roots* came out in 1976—I remember being startled by the title, the very word I used (I thought privately) to describe my own impulse to "go back" to Prague the year before, in 1975. Seeking your roots was in the air of the mid-seventies—to locate whatever *there* was still there, not only for the descendants of slaves, but those of serfs, peasants, whatever we would have been in our various versions of whichever old country our genetic code hailed from. In my case, the serving class.

How strange, then, that I never searched out my grandmother's village, never sought my grandfather's "people." I'd absorbed, without realizing it, the fact that roots are not meant to be found. They're buried. Anyway, my roots were deep enough in St. Paul—where else? It was the Great World I was lugging my blue backpack to find, not some long-lost relative.

But once past Cheb, on the dismal train to the smudged gold of Prague, I had stepped through the looking glass—not into "the Great World," as I had longed for it on the night desk of the *Pioneer Press*. This was the Other World. The other side. Our opposite, our opposition.

It was what I had left my editing job to see. Not, after all, "the old country," but the flip side of the current coin of the age. This was no root, only the bleak flower bred of blighted peacetime. The American postwar affluence that had benefited even the children of the working class (me) showed its other side now in depresso Prague, where people lined up on a street corner by a makeshift vegetable stand, hoping to score its only product—arthritic knobs of kohlrabi. Passing by in the rattling tram, glimpsing a woman at the end of the queue, wan with care, gazing wistfully at misshapen carrots on an outdoor market table—I was shocked, strangely ashamed of the wealth I hadn't realized I came from. Was I one of *the rich* after all? Repellent thought.

I first arrived in Prague the day the Americans gave up the ghost in Vietnam—April 30, 1975. The pictures went swiftly around the world: helicopters whirling up and away from the roof of the white French colonial American embassy in Saigon, desperate evacuees hanging from the struts like aerialists, leaving the city that, within twenty-four hours of the *twack-twack* of the helicopters' lifting off the embassy's flat roof, became and remains Ho Chi Minh City.

Those photographs penetrated everywhere, even behind

the Iron Curtain as I solemnly called my location, where I sat in a tatty art nouveau *kavarna,* ordering burnt coffee and pretending to smoke a cigarette.

At the time "no one," as people said, went to Prague or to the shrouded capitals of Eastern Europe (people routinely said "Eastern Europe" though Prague is, was, and always will be farther west than Vienna). A visa was required, and visas, it was understood, were hard to come by for someone traveling alone, without tour guide or group, without affiliation of some kind. I had written on the visa application line for occupation "School Teacher," which I wasn't, instead of "Writer," which I alone considered myself to be. In fact, having quit my radio job, I was unemployed. The visa came through.

Maybe those Saigon pictures were published speedily in Prague because the Communist regime was glad to report the news: Americans fleeing in disarray, Americans *losing.* The day I'm returning to must have been early May, a few days after the American defeat—which even now we don't call defeat. *We pulled out*—that's the noncommittal term we use to describe it still. I spent much of my several weeks in Prague that first trip sitting in that café or in others equally shabby and satisfying. The lilacs were in flower on Petřín Hill. When I walked on Kampa island by the Vltava, the chestnut blossoms dropped all around me like bits of blood-stained tissue. May flowers.

I had never seen a chestnut before, I had never seen a European capital, I didn't speak the language of the place, and I knew no one. I bore my big blue backpack like a penitential burden, no credit card, a small hoard of traveler's checks I tended with fetishistic care to pay for dark stews I ate in crummy restaurants frequented by Gypsies (not yet "Romany") or in smoky cafés where I made a meal of heavily sugared coffee. I was alone in that absolute way of untried youth and real travel that causes details—spring blossoms, a faded café—to churn with significance. I felt poetic every single second.

This, roughly, was the situation, inner and outer, as I sat in the Obecní Dům *kavarna*—Municipal House coffeehouse— a little less than seven years after the Warsaw Pact troops had rumbled across the Czech border into the streets of Prague and into my hand in the UPI room at the *St. Paul Pioneer Press.*

It's possible I wasn't aware until somewhat later that my country was no longer at war, the very war I had protested so hotly and proudly the length of my twenties. My college boyfriend had been a draft resister (*draft dodger*—my dental student brother), and gone to prison for almost a year, where I had visited him every permitted three weeks, sitting at a table set low so you couldn't reach across it. *No kissing! No touching!*

And of course I was not aware that this 1975 day in Saigon, half a world away from my perch at an art nouveau outpost behind the Iron Curtain, would be marked as I am marking it now, over forty years later, as the first day in the decline of what until then had seemed the inevitable and eternal ascension of my imperial but nonetheless vastly appealing country and its hot-dog culture. You can't remember everything, and I don't remember that. This is how memory works: not as transcription but as an attempt—as an essay is an attempt (and this is an essay)—to locate meaning between the irretrievable *then* and the equally unfathomable *now*.

I do remember—and knew I would remember—the flimsy red-flecked chestnut blossoms and the eloquent café smoke that conveyed, I was sure, much lyric intel for me to decode. Pull out the notebook and describe. Which I did, wherever that notebook is now, wherever that fervent description lies, the aging non-acid-free pages inexorably deconstructing my breathless prose.

I had purchased the notebook from a surly clerk in a poorly lit Prague *papírnictví*, a state shop that offered notebooks and toilet paper side by side according to the flat-footed marketing model of the socialist retail sales mind. Paper is paper—for writing poems, for wiping bottoms. I believe I noted that detail. I was beginning to trust the intelligence of details. It was the beginning of becoming a writer.

I sat at a banquette in the Obecní Dům *kavarna*, the seat made of leather the color of a roan stallion, brittle, cracked here and there, just as I expected it to be and approved: old *Mitteleuropa*. Behind me the banquette rose to a wooden railing. Above it a beveled mirror. The whole wall of the great room alternated these panels of dim mirror with mosaic panels composed of tiny tiles, romantic scenes of peasant life by Alphonse Mucha—winsome girls with opulent bosoms fastening up sheaves of wheat, a young man in a cocked hat sporting a feather flourish, a rook fastened to his gloved arm.

They were figures from the first decade of the twentieth century, public art in the art nouveau style that some decades later would be reconfigured elsewhere in the city in harsh rectilinear lines representing valiant workers of the machine age, a stolid socialist fantasy set in opposition to the luscious curves of this lazier art nouveau iconography. The glazed glow of the tiles overflowed with bouquets of intricate flowers. Ornament and decoration cascaded, pastel and jewel tones predominated—all viewed through the blue-gray of the place's primer coat of smoke that delved still deeper into Central European history.

Waiters in formal attire, dour-faced and balletic, threaded their way through the crowded room, each oval tray outfitted with cup and saucer, and a mingy paper napkin reminiscent of the toilet paper ranked on the stationery store shelves by the notebooks.

Most of the clientele were students, interspersed with tables of pensioners dressed in the sagging good lines of their once fashionably tailored First Republic haberdashery. Hats abounded on the elderly heads, gracious manners and low murmurs floated around the tables of these former citizens of the Masaryk republic who had lived through the various betrayals of their century. The students, many African or Arab from socialist or "non-aligned" states, spoke Czech in staccato accents, taking their free educations in the only Europe they had a chance for, laughing, bending over engineering problems in their big textbooks, moving from table to table as if in a dorm lounge.

It was the danky deep of the Cold War, but this May was also (as garish red-and-yellow placards and banners hoisted over streets and soot-grimed buildings barked) the thirtieth anniversary of the Liberation of Prague by "our Soviet brothers."

Everything in Prague seemed ruined, lost, or at least damaged. Hence the high poetry quotient. But the Obecní Dům *kavarna* also winked an ironic wink—that wild art nouveau excess, the glints of gold in the grimy mosaics, the happy and entirely unnecessary creamy feel-good art, the invitation to laziness—it was all a rueful Czech rebuke to the brittle demagoguery of the Husák regime that had its boot on the country's neck since the Prague Spring of 1968 had been trashed.

There was no imagining what lay ahead: November 1989, the collapse of the regime that would bring about, among other more fundamental changes, the temporary closure of this *kavarna* for several years of massive reconstruction so it could reopen to cater to the new world order—ourselves in massive, hard-currency-spending tourist droves who would take the Mucha mosaics, thanks, but hold the unfiltered cigarette smoke.

In April 1989, Václav Havel was in jail (again—this time for laying flowers at the site of the self-immolation of Jan Palach, the philosophy student who protested the Warsaw Pact invasion with his life). By December 1989, Havel was president of the country. Crazy. Not possible to imagine in 1975—or even a week before the regime collapsed in November 1989.

None of that could be imagined in 1975 because the most curious aspect of the Cold War standoff was that both sides thought the Curtain was, truly, Iron. A metallic fact that would never rust, never flake away. The blackest magic of the Cold War in retrospect was that people accepted it as permanent—with the exception, of course, of the only alternative scenario: the apocalypse of atomic war that shivered everyone's timbers. That scary alternative no doubt contributed to the illusion of permanence in the stalemate of those forty-some postwar years. If the only possible other thing is annihilation, the mind accepts without hesitation an eternity of stasis.

In those Cold War days, the whole juicy art nouveau business of the Obecní Dům *kavarna* was held together by nothing more substantial than the grimy smoke of ages from three hundred years of the Hapsburg Empire, through the First Republic's scant twenty years and the Nazi occupation, to now—almost thirty years of stale gloomy-Gus socialism.

You didn't just sit in this murky place—you were slightly levitated off the cracked leather on a billow of historical ash, the smoke of national humiliation and endurance bearing you up, eyes smarting. I bought my coffee, a pack of cigarettes, and set up shop with my notebook and my ardor. I was finally down the rabbit hole of history after a youth atop the stainless steel of American self-idealization and historical amnesia.

I was determined to describe what was before me. I felt powerfully alone and in charge of things. Even—especially—my language belonged only to me in this place where I never heard it spoken. Czech, though the language of my grandmother who had lived with us, was not my language. My attempts to learn it had only persuaded me of the revenge possible to the small nation.

It seemed I was the only American in Prague. Not possibly true, but it felt that way amid the busloads of Bulgarian and Ukrainian factory workers carted to a fellow worker state for their holiday and the small bands of West Germans driving over the border in their Mercedes, slouching around the hotel bars in their furs, coming for the music and cheap beer. I had never felt—and never felt again—so surely that a world lay before me and required my descriptive efforts.

Strange that I would assume that describing in my notebook a smoky café abandoned by the rest of "the free world" would somehow be an act of historical documentation, useful to others. But that was what I was doing—describing the *kavarna* with a ballpoint thick with poetic ink—when he approached my table, my watchtower on this other world that, I saw in an instant, was not his world either.

I don't remember his name. Or rather, I never mastered it in our brief encounter (he repeated it more than once, carefully, courteously, thoughtful of my incomprehension). And then I was too embarrassed to ask again. So, not forgotten—never absorbed.

He had detached himself from a group of students (all male) at a table not far from mine. A foreign student—I understood that immediately, as I looked up to see his chiseled Omar Sharif face bending toward me. Handsome, big soft animal eyes, a natural eagerness overlaid with winning shyness—all that in an instant. Not the shyness that requires tending and coaxing—his was the shyness of good manners, of not wanting to intrude while wanting, very much, to intrude. I felt—I was meant to feel—flattered and intrigued. Would I mind if he joined me?

God help me, I minded. For all my backpack toting, see-the-world bravado, I was paralyzed by homegirl habits, a deep provincialism that had already morphed on my first big trip into a phony Woman Writing Alone in cafés. I thought of myself as a fly on the wall, not a girl to be picked up. *Are you a lover or a fighter?* they ask in the Marine Corps. I knew I was a fighter—that is, a writer. And yet . . .

It was impossible not to smile back at him. And he was speaking English. English, my true home, my only friend. I closed the notebook and turned to face him, glad to hear my language, though inwardly fearful. I looked at the table where his friends sat—maybe he'd come over on a dare. But no, they were busy with their engineering text. He seemed to be on his own. And he seemed to like me.

I liked him too. Right away and for no reason. Well, he was outrageously handsome, but that, in my odd little feminist book, could have worked against him. I liked him because he seemed so unreservedly to like me, and because he seemed . . . free. I liked the inner eagerness I sensed too, eagerness for nothing in particular, just life itself, the next thing. Which at the moment was me. Come to think of it, I liked him a lot.

What did we talk about? Hydrology comes faintly forward as a memory trace. He was probably studying hydrology at Charles University. He laughed when he spoke of his studies, as if hydrology were comic, but there it was. He said he had had to learn Czech, and shrugged his shoulders as if giving room in his brain to this otherwise unusable language were just another of life's comic turns. I liked him, I think now, because he didn't have a depressed nerve in his beautiful body. My boyfriends had been, thus far, poetically morose. He took life as it came. He would be fun.

We were still of an age to ask immediately about our families—mother and father, sisters (of course he had several—that ease with girls), brothers. That took some time. It seemed his family was scattered all over the place, his siblings mostly in other parts of the Soviet empire doing what he was doing—studying, improving their lot. I had only a brother, a dentist, to offer, a mother and father in Minnesota. Minnesota? He'd heard of it, he said immediately. But that was probably his good manners speaking.

I allowed that I was—or rather, I wanted to be—a writer. Novels? he asked eagerly. Poetry, I said. Ah!—and I sensed that *Ah!* meant even better than novels. He would like to read one of my poems, he said. I demurred, but I liked that he asked. Later, I said.

He smiled. He liked "later."

His friends had left their table without saying goodbye, without looking our way. Good. I was beginning to feel the wallflower me fade from the scene, some other self lunging forward like one of the Mucha girls on the walls around us, creamy gardenias in my hair, eyelids at half-mast. What my mother called the come-hither look. It was understood we would have dinner somewhere nearby, though nothing had been said to confirm this.

But we didn't rise to go. We were happy, we didn't feel like moving. We had all the time in the world. Besides, then and now the coffeehouses of Central Europe invite timelessness, the illusion of long life and endless talk. Why move? Why do anything? The intellectual life of the early twentieth century that remains a dream state—newspapers on wooden dowels, hours frittered in conversation—was strong in the air.

I still think if we'd left the *kavarna* and walked down Dlouhá to some dumpy *pivnice* for a dumpling-and-gravy dinner, if we had not made the particular left turn in our conversation we made at that table in the *kavarna*—if, if, if.

But we sat on, happy in our timelessness. I asked him (because it suddenly occurred to me I had not asked) where he was from. He had asked or rather confirmed early on that I was an American. He had pretended to know where Minnesota was. He had a brother in California. But now I asked where he was from.

From nowhere, he said. *People like me are from nowhere.* He became, in an instant, a different person, not the eager, easy face I had so uncharacteristically permitted to sit at my table. A shroud of grief descended on the beautiful dark features. *I'm Palestinian,* he said. And waited a bit fearfully for me to respond, as if I might turn on him for this admission.

Something decisive had been said. I got that, something grave and immense, unbridgeable. Something I could not describe in the notebook that lay closed on the table between us. I didn't know what the word he had pronounced signified, and I sensed that not to know what "Palestinian" was indicated that I, not he, was the nobody in this conversation. I was instinctively aware that I could not let him know I had no idea what a "Palestinian" was. Something out of the Bible?

It's hard to believe now that I, who fancied myself "political" with my antiwar passion, my feminist this and that, my civil rights talk (I had taken the train to Chicago to hear Martin Luther King speak—wrote it up for the paper), my general Sixties Generation assumptions and "positions"—that this person, me myself, did not know what he was talking about. There was Israel and there were Arabs over there and they were fighting—or not fighting but not friends. I knew nothing, nothing. This wasn't the World. This was the Unknown.

He was speaking ardently now. I must understand that his people (he said "my people," a deep affirming designation of solidarity I had never heard an American use to describe our fellow citizens) were good people, ordinary people (he wasn't ordinary to me). *We only want a home,* he said. *You must understand this.*

I had no idea what he was talking about.

The panic that coursed through me was the panic of cowardly ignorance. I had to *get out.* Get away. No dinner in a little *hospoda* for him and me. No poem "later." No Omar Sharif eyes gazing into mine, his face coming nearer, nearer in the dark.

I knew nothing, nothing about the world that he assumed any conscious being would know. My roots—ha! I had come to Prague after everyone in my lineage was dead or gone. I had no roots. I was an American. I had only dreaminess and the holy scripture of my notebook to affirm my illusions, my basket of plucked details, my descriptions. Most of all, my cool blue American passport, my traveler's checks, my imperial security. My ignorance.

I gathered up my gear from the campsite I'd made of the table—postcards, map, book (Kundera in English, which like a visitor from First Amendment land I had showily brought as my reading material), the notebook. *I have to go,* I said.

He looked confused. Had he read me wrong? I had seemed

so sympathetic. We were having such a wonderful talk. Was it that he was Palestinian? Was I—he hadn't thought of this—was I Jewish?

No, I muttered. *Catholic. I just have to go, can't stay, can't go to dinner.*

If I were Jewish, I thought much later, I would have known what he was talking about.

Please, he said, pleading in the word. He reached across the table, touched my arm. *Please*—he wanted me to convey to my people (my people!) how simple were the hopes and dreams of his people. *Please take our story back to your people—you're a writer.*

A smoke-grimed Prague café, filled with foreign students from the "non-aligned" countries of Africa and the Middle East. This one a Palestinian who presents himself to me with a poetic and ardent face, asking me to *understand—we only want a home like everyone else.* Go home and write that. *You're a writer.*

What do you do with such moments, flashes that don't even amount to episodes, bare proto-encounters? Another tattered vignette, tossed in the unsorted shoebox. That's what I did. I wrote the book about my travels to Prague, but he isn't in it. The *kavarna* is there, heavily described, but no Palestinian.

But here he is, sprung from the dark of his unwritten chapter. I was so grotesquely ignorant that even though I found him adorable, I could not continue our tentative flirtation. It would come out that I didn't know what a Palestinian was. And this, I sensed, was a terrible abyss. I could not comprehend his grief. I never felt so American.

Now, all these years later, having had plenty of time to learn what a Palestinian is, I sit across Vlasta's table from my old friend Anna, waiting for dinner, both of us sipping Becherovka. Anna has done more good in the world than anyone I know, braving impossible situations, harrowing conditions in Africa, Bangladesh, traveling as a doctor, her passion and curiosity for other people and other cultures still evergreen in spite of a botched hip operation (she walks now with a cane), a bad heart, a body broken by care for others and carelessness for herself.

We have had "words" about Israel and Palestine. Also about the Syrian refugees who, she says with dismay, are "overwhelming" Europe. I am now full of feeling for Palestinians. I'm a veritable expert on Palestine and Palestinians. Israel—of course Israel, I say. Of course. But what about the Palestinians, what about the *occupation* of their land?

No, no, no. The Jews must have Israel. Don't I know what they went through? As if I hadn't heard about the Holocaust. "My" president Jimmy Carter, she says accusingly, had no business comparing the Palestinian situation to apartheid. She knows Israel, she has been there. So have I, I cry, twice! Travel, even tourism, as the tarnished badge of authority.

Back and forth we went at it the night before in the dark, lying on our adjoining cots in Vlasta's bedroom (Vlasta herself camped out neatly on her settee, having no worries about the Middle East, plotting the next Central European meal like a military action, the next day's hike into wine country).

Both of us admit in the morning, sheepishly, that we couldn't get to sleep after our—well, fight. It wasn't a discussion, not even an argument. A fight. She wins—or I let her win. In my experience, a Czech always wins any political argument, even if it's about American politics. It is impossible for any Czech I've met to believe an American has the necessary gravitas to know anything about politics. We are naïve, we are a nation of appealing (often) or dangerous (more often) simpletons. It's exhausting to engage in political discussion with someone who has not only lived in the backstreets of the impoverished world, but has the lived experience of her own brutalized twentieth-century history at home, her life history radiating authority from wartime babyhood to this tough and tenderhearted woman limping along gamely with her cane, always ready to show me her country. *You see, you see?* she says, delighted whenever I appreciate something—cherry trees bending with fruit on a country road, Rožmberk Castle in south Bohemia, folk songs in a village *hospoda,* everyone knowing all the words, the solidarity of national music, the wizened landscape of north Bohemia, soured by the ruinous land use policies of the socialist regime. She insists I see it all, year by year since the end of the Cold War.

I knew nothing in 1975 in the smoky *kavarna.* Apparently I know a different kind of nothing now in Vlasta's new world order *panalak* apartment.

We resolve this impasse as we always do: gorgeous meal, then a long walk. Not a hike, but a saunter through Znojmo, Vlasta in the lead. Summer dusk, and we head into the old town. It's not far away, and it's more beautiful than I remember from earlier visits. This may be because we have the old town to ourselves, walking the cobbled streets, stopping at a baroque castle lit by a streetlamp and glowing, on to this church, another, finding glorious "prospects," as eighteenth-century travelers called scenic views from their coaches. Much has been restored and repainted, returned since 1989 to its *Mitteleuropa* jewel-like pastels, the Hapsburg mustard yellow prominent. We look out over the dark sash of the river Djye, below the green hills where yet another church is perched, named for Saint Hippolyte, whoever he was, though apparently a big enough saint to earn a cathedral on the distant eminence. Also across the river a smaller, more "Eastern" (Slavic) chapel, its onion dome belonging to some lesser saint. Still farther off, the raised line of a toy railroad arced from our side of the river to the other. The train to Austria. For most of Vlasta's life, and Anna's, the unbridgeable bridge dividing East from West. Now just another branch line of the EU, no passport required, no guard tower. Come and go as you wish—except for me, the American. I must show my passport.

On our return to the apartment, moving from one lozenge of dim light to the next, streetlamp by streetlamp, we pass the gymnasium where Gregor Mendel taught for one unhappy year in 1849.

Mendel had entered the Augustinian novitiate at St. Thomas monastery in Brno in 1843, a decision he made to free himself, he wrote, "from the bitter struggle for existence." He had been studying science and philosophy at the university in Olomouc, and it is not clear if this *bitter struggle* was the plight of a poor boy trying to find his way in academic life without money or support, or something more coiled within. It may have been a question of psychological struggle, the oppression of some private fear or worry.

He was first assigned to give spiritual aid to people in a Brno hospital, but the sight of so much suffering pulverized his own spirit, and he took to his bed for a month. He was famously "timid." Or perhaps he had an excess of empathy, a gentleness without any protective personal shield to allow him to act on this fellow-feeling in the face of human misery. He asked to be given another assignment. He suggested teaching. For this he needed more university training. That meant, eventually, he had to mount the barricades of oral exams.

A series of unhappy years followed for the exam-phobic Mendel, whose timidity turned to stark terror in the face of performance. He tried twice to gain the certificate to allow him to teach in the high school system of the Austro-Hungarian Empire. After his second failure before the examiners in Vienna, he gave up, accepted the humiliating (or at least humbling) position of substitute teacher, settling eventually back into the damp Augustinian abbey in Brno where at least there was a lovely garden and greenhouse. Here he lived the rest of his life.

Mendel was destined to remain in the backwaters of science, picking up the slack when someone on the regular faculty got sick or was away. But then he was from a backwater, a village in Silesia where he was born into a peasant family. Humility was his native realm.

Yet everyone in his village seems to have seen that this peasant boy had intellectual ability—his sister gave him her dowry so he could attend university. His entrance into monastic life may have been a way for a poor boy to further his education. Not only a poor boy, but also a profoundly shy boy (his baffling failure of his oral exams surely was evidence of social panic). Was he a man of faith or was religion merely a choice of convenience? Theology in the service of biology suggests that he wasn't much of a believer.

That's how our age tends to see it.

But here may be another modern reading of an earlier century's struggle that's more about us than about Mendel. We may limit the notion of "belief" in this secular age as Colette limited "romantic friendship" to sexual behavior (of course thinking she was liberating it). Faith in our time can seem like signing on the dotted line of a prefab doctrine composed of absurdities.

But another version: faith isn't what you think, what you "believe." It's what you do. Religion may be more practical than our secular age imagines. Language holds on to this notion, covertly. The question, for example, isn't *are you a believing Catholic?* It's *are you a practicing Catholic?* Language instinctively gets it—what you "believe" is less important, in fact becomes mere speculation or brittle dogma, in the presence of a way of life.

The Ladies of Llangollen devised their System—a thing of daily living beauty to them. So too the solitude of monastic life could offer not just a free education to a poor boy from the sticks, but an appealing order, gently shaping life, grounding it for an essentially contemplative endeavor that required not intellectual fireworks but profound patience. This daily domestic order would have great appeal to a teeming mind, one shy of the grit of social maneuvering, lacking the sharp elbows of ambition, loving instead the things of the earth, the focus on the immediate growing world, the daily round of life. Time's seasonal shape. Monastic life is, among other things, profoundly domestic. A lot of bread baking, honey gathering, wine making in that way of life.

Mendel was a natural gardener, as attentive to his patch of pea plants as the Ladies to their Shrubbery, if far more inquisitive about the inner workings of those pea plants than they were of their boxwood.

Darwin, who trained originally in theology, struggled with the relation of religion and science. He remains our model of that enduring opposition. Mendel, on the other hand, lived in religion, apparently without significant intellectual struggle. In time he even became the abbot of his monastery. Religion was his day job, his avocation in science a thoroughly focused fascination, and quite naturally fitting into the rest of his life. The pea plants were part of creation. No problem, as we say.

Mendel's contribution to science, unlike Darwin's, didn't stray into theoretical matters. Yet his study of the reproductive patterns of the edible pea (green versus yellow, smooth skinned versus wrinkled) revealed the inner workings of cellular evolution that remained vexingly elusive to Darwin. Mendel's conception of the gene was perhaps the greatest modern scientific act of the imagination, right up there with

Einstein's theory of relativity, on the cellular rather than cosmic scale.

On the drive to Znojmo, Anna and I had spent an afternoon in Brno at the Mendel museum housed in the old Augustinian abbey where he'd lived, now part of Masaryk University. I tried to follow the intricacies of his meticulous notations mounted on the displays, his careful transcription of peapod family life, the spidery lines connecting small circles, dividing, combining, reconfiguring change and chance over vegetal generations.

But what I took away was not a sudden understanding of the science, any more than I had comprehended genetics from the unit in high school biology (*and girls—Gregor Mendel was a monk, a contemplative*). What I saw in his charting was clear evidence not of genetic theory, but of patience, tenderness. A gentle soul, a gardener. I wandered off to the gift shop and bought a coffee mug (pea green, naturally) with the museum's peapod logo, and sat on a stone bench in the abbey-museum courtyard. Out with the notebook, reminding myself once again about my grandmother's kitchen garden, her perennial border of heavy-headed maroon and white peonies, my grandfather behind his toolshed, training green beans up a rattan lattice, tying off the tendrils with cotton twine. My florist father hoodwinking Easter lilies and poinsettias to bloom in perfect time for the holidays. Care and tending, the pacific life of gardening, the Edenic assignment that predated laboring "by the sweat of your brow."

Mendel read Darwin in a German translation of *Origin of Species*. It appears, however, that Darwin did not know Mendel's work. He came heartbreakingly close to reading Mendel's paper on his pea experiments (published in an obscure Moravian agricultural journal). Mendel's paper is mentioned in an omnibus review of recent work of the time. Darwin made notes on his copy of this review, curiously skipping over the mention of Mendel's paper without a marginal note. It's possible, had Darwin read this modest document with its careful study of pea plant patterns, that genetics would have been a nineteenth-century discovery—and considered the capstone of Darwin's remarkable career. Perhaps.

But, as geneticists now marvel, it was not until 1900 that Mendel's work was "discovered," finally seen for what it is—the key to cellular life and the mysterious workings of heredity. This was sixteen years after Mendel had died in relative obscurity, known as the abbot of his Augustinian congregation, not as the father of genetics—a word not even coined in his lifetime.

As a monk, Mendel passed his days within the liturgy of Hours, wedded to the seasonal world in spiraling patterns of great resonance, prayers belonging not to any creed or dogma, not even to Christianity. These ancient texts of the Hebrew Psalms structure the Western monastic day, season, year as they have since the desert fathers.

Mendel's was a way of life, then, organized by poetry. A life never more than a few hours distant from the Psalms, poems that form the genetic code of Western lyricism, its grief and fury, its exultation. For the West, the Psalms are the enduring communal trace of the experience of being alive, passed on and on, over generations in ancient cries and murmurs, mutating over time, moving from one religion to another into monastic chant, finally into lyric poetry. Between the sacred lyric and the secular lyric there is no argument. They form the same enterprise, the full range of living consciousness from rage to jubilation running along the lifeline of the West. Kinship. Heredity.

Eventually, after Mendel became the abbot of his monastery, he abandoned his plant experiments as he shouldered the administration of the monastic household. He had presented his findings—in a characteristically obscure regional journal. We do not know if he was disappointed in the ripple his work did not make.

Mendel was sixty-one when he died in Brno in 1884. And then was forgotten. Even the fact that Leoš Janáček played the organ at his funeral is not a sign of his eminence: Janáček wasn't *Janáček* yet, just a young Moravian musician with a church organist job, his operas and the *Sinfonietta* years ahead, his own humble researches into Moravian folk song, the genetic code of his music, all in the future, part of the twentieth century, not the nineteenth, as Mendel's work too ends up resurrected in the twentieth century. Playing for Mendel's funeral was simply Janáček's job. As being abbot was Mendel's.

We're eating very slowly now, meditatively. The last night in Znojmo, after another big day in the countryside—a castle, a walk through vineyards, that most elegantly arranged farmland, retaining as no other cropland does the sense of a garden. Anna insisted we take a detour in her little car to see the border between Moravia and Austria, a patch of the Iron Curtain left standing as a "cultural marker" with a national parks insignia on a sign in a broad swath of tall grass overlooking open terrain. East on this side, West on the other. The barbed-wire fencing (once electrified, now just rusting) led to the guard tower, a weathered wooden perch on stilts, not so different from a deer stand in Minnesota. There was a *hospoda* and a *kavarna* on the road where people stopped for a beer or coffee after walking up the gravel pathway to the guard tower. Older couples, quiet, standing still, looked across to Austria, the formerly illicit landscape. And young families, the children held by the hand, the situation explained to them, and then let to run free up the path, begging to climb up the rickety wooden tower. No, no, that was not allowed, the parents yelled, their voices caught and blown westward by the wind.

Did people get shot trying to escape across the border? *Ano, ano,* Anna said. Yes, that happened. Vlasta nodded, turned away. But the suicide numbers were much higher. Why would someone commit suicide while trying to escape to the West? No, it wasn't the ones fleeing. It was the soldiers told to shoot them. They were the suicides. Many. They chose young conscripts, not real soldiers—who didn't want such a job. And told them to shoot anyone getting past the electrified wire. Many of these boys could not bring themselves to do that. We stood by the barbed wire, looking out at the landscape identical to the one on our side. The children were tearing around the guard tower, a game of tag, their parents calling to get back to the car.

And then we were back on the road, off to a picnic site and wine tasting on the edge of—what was it the edge of? Some hidden glen between forest and meadow, a stream-fed pond nearby, down a pathway after we abandoned Anna's little mixmaster of a car. I would never be able to find the place again. It lives in memory with the improbability of a fairy tale.

There, in this secluded spot, families, lovers, old couples, friends (Vlasta, Anna, me) spread out blankets on the ground before a makeshift little stage where several men, each with a glass of white wine by his chair, sat with instruments—accordion, banjo, sax—and played their hearts out. Dixieland jazz, a Czech specialty, no one knows why. Jazz was illicit—therefore a form of freedom—during the Cold War. It endures now as part of the Czech songbook. Sitting in that mushroom-loving landscape, drinking local white wine, I didn't find it odd. Dixieland seemed very Czech.

A table was set up with bottles of local wines from a nearby *sklep* (wine cellar). For a small charge we were given a wineglass, and went up to the table, tasting one white wine after another, Vlasta pursing her lips, swirling her glass. She asked, chin raised in inquiry, which did I like best? I sensed my answer would reveal the quality of my mind—the palate is a kind of intelligence, evidence of discernment. I swirled the pale gold in my glass, sipped, swallowed. Then the next wine, the next. You mustn't rush this. I had no idea which was best. I went back for the second, the *ryzlink vlašský,* pointed to it. Vlasta nodded. *Ano*—yes. I had chosen correctly. *You see, you see,* Anna cried—always her cri de coeur when I had understood something, when I *got* it.

Finally back at the apartment, the last supper, and Vlasta has outdone herself in the offhand way of a master indulging the audience with an encore. It is the season of the *meruňka*— apricot time. It's unclear when, exactly, she had time to make the dough for the little pillows of these dumplings, when she managed to buy the apricots, though we passed many hand-lettered *Meruňky* signs along the narrow, tree-lined roads we drove to the picnic site in the afternoon.

She pours melted butter over the ivory lumps in our shallow soup plates, then a brief snowstorm of sugar and crumbled white cheese, dry and salty. We pierce the puffery of the dough with big dessert spoons. Out comes the yellow-orange fruit, melting from the dumpling's creamy white, like a perfectly coddled egg. *Oh my,* I say. They both beam at me. *You see, you see,* Anna says, as if I have finally seen the light she keeps trying to show me. My pleasure is proof that, in spite of everything I get wrong, maybe I'm learning after all what matters in life.

Back home after the Moravian interlude with Mendel. Or really with Anna and Vlasta, the time-wasting idyll Anna says is left over from the sequestered days of the Cold War when nobody could go anywhere, when ambition (outside the Party) was impossible, when all that was left of personal freedom was to enjoy yourself in the littleness of the moment, wine in the countryside, perfecting the apricot dumpling, frittering the day with friends stuck as you were stuck. Real friends, dreamers—the people you knew had integrity.

That was the through-the-looking-glass sensation I'd experienced in Prague during the Cold War, and hadn't understood at the time. Beyond all the obvious differences we in the West loved to tote up—our freedoms, their oppression—there was this beguiling *whatever* quality to social relations in Czecho, people hanging out, listening to music, cooking, slow coffee-drinking afternoons skimming into wine-drinking evenings, late, late into the night. The *chuta* life—cottage life—weekends tending gardens, lying low. Living. Of course the new world market order has changed all that, but it's still there, still part of the sense of time and how to spend it. That is, waste it.

I always think I can bring it back with me, as if after a trip to Spain or Italy, you could import the siesta culture into the cold North. Can't be done. It's not about taking a nap in the middle of the day. It's about—well, that's the question, that's what keeps me going back not only to Czecho, but to Montaigne, that *lax, drowsy* man in his tower.

So back home—with Montaigne as I absurdly think, as if he were riding shotgun with me wherever I go. The big lug of his essays I carry around, the audio version on my iPhone in my pocket, plugged into my ear as I walk the dog. I'm still hesitating to visit his château, still in schoolgirl mode, doing my homework—I even try reading some of the *Essais* in the original French, I reread the Donald Frame biography. I suppose it's an obsession, an attempt to find, across the maw of centuries, some kind of explanation for the kinship I feel.

I keep coming back to music—that lute player following him around the château of his childhood. No lutes in my childhood, but there is my Czech father with his determination to fill my mind with music too.

Piano. Originally *pianoforte.* But by the twentieth century the loud register had been dropped from the word. The idea of *quiet and slow and soft*—the Italian word *piano*—was all that was left to carry the whole bulky piece of musical furniture. Montaigne never knew one, never heard one. He was a century too early for the piano. His father, Pierre, would certainly have been an early adopter.

In any case, he gave his boy a very *pianissimo* childhood.

Pierre also employed a German who knew no French and "was very highly paid" to be the boy's Latin tutor. He wanted to be sure his son's native tongue was the language of classical Rome. Even the servants were required to address the boy only in Latin.

"It is wonderful how everyone profited from this," Montaigne reports in an essay recounting his early education. "My father and mother learned enough Latin in this way to understand it . . . as did also the servants who were most attached to my service. Altogether, we Latinized ourselves so much that it overflowed all the way to our villages on every side. . . . I was over six before I understood any more French or Perigordian than Arabic."

This Latin immersion was contrived, by the relatively uneducated but doting Pierre, so that his son would learn the international language of the age "without artificial means, without a book, without grammar or precept, without the whip and without tears." The only way to learn, Montaigne always believed. Perfect for the *sluggish, lax, drowsy* child.

In his lethargy the boy displayed the requirements of the particular kind of writer he became—disregard for received knowledge and a mandarin disdain for received form, coupled with acute observation and the punch and fluency of expression on the fly. He found his métier early—the essay.

Except the métier didn't yet exist. He found his talent, then. And awaited its purpose and its form. Waiting suited his temperament after all—*sluggish, lax, drowsy.* As it would suit the voluptuous unspooling of his apparently artless art, a mind awakened every morning not by command, not even by thought, but by a fugitive strand of music.

Piano, piano! The entreaty of the long-suffering Bernard Weiser. Not a noun, not invoking the elephantine instrument I was meant to master, but a cautionary adverb. We sat side by side, he at his grand, I at mine, both of us enduring the weekly lesson in his cramped Scott Hall studio. *Gently, gently!* Every week he urged me down from my wrestling matches with Bach, with Scarlatti—he counted on them to tame me. But nothing could gentle my melodramatic relation to music.

It was my single year as a music major, the year the jig was finally up. My high school musicianship (much indulged, much inflated) gave way in college to the truth of my mediocrity, and late in my freshman year I skulked off to Vincent Hall, joining all the other lost souls in the morose building the English Department shared with Mortuary Science.

But think of the years of piano practice that preceded that final descent from music into language, into sentences and paragraphs. Into this.

All the years alone in little rooms with music. The little living room on Linwood where the baby grand crouched in its shiny chestnut coat, the biggest thing, except for our Ford, that we owned. But even more, the studio cells of my girls' school, the cloistered nuns of the old French order presiding serenely, where one day a week in the refectory (not "lunch-room" or "cafeteria") we spoke only French. *Puis-je avoir les cornichons, si vous plaît, ma soeur?* And the little sour pickles in a cut-glass dish were handed over with an approving smile. *Bien sûr, ma chère.*

The building, rosy brick with a soaring campanile, the nuns in their Renaissance gowns gliding from the cloister with its bewitching sign, ENCLOSURE, we students wearing our Madeleine uniforms, the entire atmosphere that the shadowy marble halls held in a fierce embrace—none of it would have been foreign to Montaigne. His religion, his nation, shades of his ancien régime.

But it's wrong to say that the embrace of the place was *fierce.* It was *piano, pianissimo.* As if lute music followed us too, up and down the worn marble staircases. The gentleness insinuated itself, wielding the power of assumption and habit, not brute might. Gentleness was the paradoxical strength of the place, the reason the word *fierce,* though inaccurate, comes to mind. There was no threat of violence in that muscle, but muscle it was. Nobody was a bully. An unchallenged chatelaine authority ruled. We, in our blue serge uniforms, formed a well-behaved vassal estate.

This *comme il faut* world, improbably transported to the Upper Midwest, gasped its last gasp with us, its social order held in the double embrace of religion and good manners, having come up the Mississippi from St. Louis after the Civil War, several founding nuns bearing in their ménage a brocade chair eventually placed in the school library and said to have been sat in by Bonaparte.

This wrought-iron gentility remained neatly caged in a leafy Victorian neighborhood of a provincial midwestern capital well past the middle of the twentieth century. In St. Paul, a city that usually thinks of itself as Irish Catholic, the oldest families, the ones who had sent their daughters to our school for generations, bore French names—DesLauriers, LaBossicrc, Villaume. I did not belong to this caste, but was admitted as a favor to my great-aunt, who as a retired state school inspector had helped the cloistered nuns earn their teaching certificates without breaching the convent wall. Aunt Aggie, she of the soulful recitation of Romantic poetry—*O for a beaker of the warm South.*

The city's earliest ancestral link was not, after all, to the pioneers of the nineteenth century who were much invoked in American history class for having "settled" Minnesota, as if they had covered it up and put it to bed. We touched further back, to seventeenth-century French fur traders, the *coureurs de bois,* the first Europeans to trespass the rivers and boreal forests of the New World. They scouted the territory only a few decades after Montaigne was affixing his final editorial notes on bits of paper glued to the margins of the endlessly revised, ever-expanding book, the only one he wrote. The book of life—his life.

The *Essais.* His attempts—to make sense of his world, even to contend with the first glimmers of ours, the reports and rumors just arriving from the fabulous New World, "the Indies" far south of North America, but still our world. The New World, as my Czech peasant grandmother also called it, having left *the old country.*

Montaigne holds a bead on the tabloid eye of his own world as it first glimpses ours. He reports and muses on the conversations he has pursued with "a man who had lived for ten or twelve years in that other world which has been discovered in our century."

Montaigne is aware of the fantasias hatched by this exotic otherness in the European mind—"I am afraid we have eyes bigger than our stomachs, and more curiosity than capacity. We embrace everything, but we clasp only wind." How tempting to believe in monsters, as they are drawn around the margins of maps of early modern cartographers.

In an effort to protect himself from credulity, Montaigne notes how carefully he chooses his informant about this new world. "Clever people observe more things and more curiously," he admits, "but they interpret them; and to lend weight and conviction to their interpretation, they cannot help altering history a little."

The first mistrustful critique of nonfiction.

The problem with such sophisticated observers, he says, is that "they never show you things as they are, but bend and disguise them according to the way they have seen them; and to give credence to their judgment and attract you to it, they are prone to add something . . . to stretch it out and amplify it."

Much better the witness he chooses as his informant—"a simple crude fellow" (*homme simple et grossier*). You must find "a man either very honest, or so simple that he has not the stuff to build up false inventions and give them plausibility; and wedded to no theory. Such was my man."

But is such *our* man? Montaigne is our witness, the first personal voice to report from the identity we claim for ourselves and keep trying to sort out—the modern self. Whatever else he proves himself to be in his pages, the Sieur de Montaigne is no simple, crude fellow.

What do we mean when we invoke "the modern," anyway? Isn't an essential aspect of the modern sensibility the imposition of personal interpretation—the very thing Montaigne is warning against? More to the point, isn't the essay, the form he invents and that fills our world with op-ed pieces and blog screeds, exactly what he claims to distrust? These "clever" people may well "observe more things and more curiously," but they do so only to "interpret" and "lend weight and conviction to their interpretation."

We're ever ready for a personal response. For us, "the personal" signals authenticity. It's modernity's primer coat of truth. Or perhaps its veneer. *What do* you *think?* we ask each other. We're asking not just for an opinion but for subjective perception, which we take for honesty. But Montaigne is vexed that these clever witnesses "never show you things as they are, but bend and disguise them according to the way they have seen them."

But isn't that the job? Saying what you see? Doesn't *the way* you see create the value of saying what you see? It's the point of attempting, trying. Of writing essays. For the secret life of an essay is to lift the veil on the process of thinking, that most intimate of acts, to reveal not a thought, but *thinking.* As he said of his project, *I don't portray being. I portray passing.* This is the evergreen quality of Montaigne's close observation, his curious notations. Not exactly the work of a reliably simple, crude fellow. It may be the reason he can seem, though he is not, "modern."

He would protest any distancing of himself from that *homme simple et grossier*. He claims a lumpen birthright. Pierre emerges again with another of his parenting theories. This one predates even the lute player and morning serenades. "The good father that God gave me," Montaigne reports "with gratitude for his goodness," saw to it that his son was "held over the baptismal font by people of the lowliest class, to bind and attach me to them."

Nor was this a mere gesture—though gestures performed in a world still awash in medieval metaphor as much as in the blood of religion were never "mere." Peasant villagers didn't just hold the baby over the baptismal font. Pierre took it further. "He sent me from the cradle to be brought up in a poor village of his and kept me there as long as I was nursing, and even longer, training me to the humblest and commonest way of life."

Pierre's idea was to let children "be formed by fortune under the laws of the common people and of nature" (*des loix populaires et naturelles*). Children should be left "to custom to train them to frugality and austerity, so that they may have rather to come down from rigorousness than climb toward it."

Pierre had "still another goal" in housing his child for his first years with peasants, away from the château (away from his mother too, perhaps—she gets short shrift and is hardly mentioned in the *Essais,* just as Montaigne barely mentions his own wife). "His notion," Montaigne says, was "to ally me with the people and that class of men that needs our help; and he considered that I was duty bound to look rather to the man who extends his arms to me than the one who turns his back on me."

All in all, Montaigne approves his father's method: "His plan," he writes, "has succeeded not at all badly." Some self-satisfaction in that voice. Montaigne admits that his tendency to devote himself to the peasants, *les petits,* may bear a touch of "vainglory" as well as "natural compassion." A patronizing note sounds—or the postmodern liberal ear cannot help hearing one. The toot of baronial benevolence. Montaigne admits it—that *vainglory* he notes.

The American ear, tuned to self-reliance, rebels, sees this as noblesse oblige, reading the *Essais* two centuries after the French Revolution. We keep dashing forward—to our many refinements, our self-regard, the exhausting mental exertions of arranging ourselves as the purpose of the past. The destination of history? Us, of course.

Montaigne writes about himself, from himself. But not quite for himself. He isn't really modern—he's about to be modern. He tilts and balances between a mind filled with stern classical moral guides—Virgil, Horace—who are quick with life for him, speaking in his ancient first language and, on the other hand, the reveals of the first-person voice. The shades of Socrates, Seneca, Ovid on one side, and then, emerging, a half-formed creature stepping into the glare of individualism, his personal voice, detached from every contrivance. That voice is the new world. His new world.

And, in time, ours.

Montaigne examines the only specimen available to him. The smear on his lab slide is himself.

What seems to interest him about those early village years is not the benevolence he feels toward *les petits*. Whatever is good—or bad—about being "prone to devote myself to *les petits*" is not worth claiming as a virtue. He wants to know his use, not his psychology. His place, not his self. Yet there is this thing called the self—this newly whetted tool.

He takes it up—the cudgel of thinking, barely nicked with personal narrative.

What strikes him about his devotion to *les petits,* as he considers it from the dark of childhood memory in his cold adult tower, is how that devotion has seeped into his political will, how it elicits balance against the sovereignty of his own side (the Catholics) in the vicious Wars of Religion that bloody the landscape. "The side I condemn [the Protestants] in our wars I will condemn more harshly when it is flourishing and prosperous; I will be somewhat reconciled to it when I see it miserable and crushed."

The weakness and vulnerability of the Protestant "other side" (note: not "the enemy") call forth not the bray of victory, but the somewhat wistful urge for harmony and reconciliation. And not only when the other side is "miserable and crushed." The question is one of balance, the equity of compassion. It draws him out of himself, from his own side to the other.

What interests Montaigne and seems to bemuse him is that he's for the underdog in all struggles, all fights. How did that happen? He looks to the raw village of his nurse and *les petits* huddled there. Did they do this to his mind, his self? Make him more empathic than he intended? For him "the other" is not nearly as other as it is, apparently, for us. His mind has not been wounded by centuries of separateness, isolation—by being first and primarily an individual. He belongs. And understands that so too do all others—they too belong, if not to his "side."

The essayist sits—he also paces—in his tower. He loafs and invites his soul—as Whitman calls this kind of work three centuries later. Montaigne can survey his entire estate, spread before him from his library where he writes and inquires of himself. His mind forms "so frivolous and vain a subject," he warns the reader on the first page of his book, it's a waste of time for anyone else to bother with it.

He is Catholic, some of his immediate relatives are Protestant. His neighbors, on either side of the religious divide, lock their châteaux, turn them into castle keeps. They await the worst, and often it comes, marauding raiders storming citadels, invading sanctuaries. Human torches flame and smoke, bowels are disgorged, the stench of holy murder everywhere.

Montaigne can see it from his tower. The smoke, the ruin. He doesn't lock his gates. He keeps his château open. It is never attacked.

He sits in his room, loafing, inviting his soul. Or wherever the words on the page come from.

But he's also off on the perilous Gascon roads, men at his side, a soldier-diplomat trusted by kings, performing shuttle diplomacy, happier on horseback than anywhere on earth, he says. He serves, when asked, as mayor of Bordeaux, he writes persuading letters, he advises and cajoles and adjudicates. The Catholic king and his retinue ride into his courtyard. They stay the night. Later the Protestant king and his men stop to parley at the château. The hospitality of Montaigne and his wife comes down through the Bordeaux records.

He threads the needle of strife with his silken thread.

Disaster averted.

Then the truce is broken. Mayhem yet again, stench rising from village to village, *les petits* scattered, the lords of the land gutted on pikes.

The Wars of Religion continue his entire lifetime. They are his world. His *piano* life, his *fortissimo* age.

The piano lessons started early, age eight—mine was another father determined to fill his child's mind with music. Soon the Sunday dinner recitals begin, aunts and uncles sitting docilely with their coffee. I'm told to go to the piano, my father pulls rosin along the bow of his violin. *How about a duet for everyone, Patricia?* We seesaw our way along Dvořák's *Humoresque #9*.

These domestic displays were only the tip of my iceberg. Hours of practice, of daydream repetition, led me along the narrow creaking corridor of my convent school, to the little cell filled up with a grand piano. The window overlooked the cloister garden, a nun drifting below, reading her breviary. Angelus time, after lunch, everyone else playing softball, screaming madly in the distance.

I could hardly wait to get to that room. Not to practice. I just played, reinscribing errors and miscues and erratic tempi. Sister Mary Louise, preternaturally patient, did what she could. I was supposed to use the metronome, but I almost never did, maddened by its pedantic tick-tocking. It was interrupting me. Interrupting what, *ma chère?*

Daydreams, the mind cantering over its landscape like an unbroken pony. The piano was a romantic sound track, not work I was doing. I was toiling elsewhere. Well, I wasn't toiling. That was the point, that was the pleasure. I was swooning. I was—as he put it—*lax, drowsy.*

Music made these travels possible. My hands moved over the keyboard, my mind went . . . anywhere it wanted to go. Paris and New York were familiar destinations, all the more vivid for knowing nothing about them, not even anyone who had seen them. I also visited, revisited, the insides of certain books—the coach Becky Sharp throws Dr. Johnson's Dictionary out of, Tennyson's flower plucked, root and all, from the crannied wall, Blake's grain of sand, Ezra Pound's petals on a wet, black bough—Sister Maria Coeli introduced all of them to us in English class.

Books pulled me, pulled me back—or maybe they pushed me forward. I circled around them, kept circling. I also had to build a case against my brother who was a bully and against my mother who sided with my brother. I had to wonder why I wasn't one of the pretty ones. Or was I? Awaiting the right person to see beneath the surface (think Jane Eyre). I was busy. I wrote poems up there in the practice room, and I kept a diary.

I didn't think of any of these sketchy bits of writing as essays. I called them nothing at all. It wasn't writing. It was me. *Ainsi, lecteur, je suis moy-mesmes la matière de mon livre.* So, reader, I am myself the material of my book. Montaigne's inaugural words are the motto of every diary.

Montaigne warned the reader against bothering to read someone else's musings—his own—even while knowing very well he was going to publish his book, offer it for sale to the public. But who has not been tempted to open a journal, a letter left on a hallway table, a postcard left face up? Montaigne knew his essays presented a fascination, even a slightly illicit one. He knew his readers perhaps better than he knew himself—as writers do, being passionate readers before they become writers. And therefore knowing what allures, what enchants.

It had a lock and a key, the first book I wrote. A red leatherette five-year diary. The lock and key were the most important part—absolute privacy, invitation to candor. A book that was a room to live in alone.

So writing was not fundamentally storytelling. It was attention. The hunting and gathering stage of civilization, the collecting of . . . what? Truth. Not "the truth" as it was purveyed in religion class, swanning forward, immutable, grandiose, the brittle carapace of dogma holding it aloft. This other truth was fluid, the mote in the eye, the sniff of the nose, the stroke of the hand reaching out. It was the truth of noticing, the patchwork of reality. It had no superstructure, no organization. Its order was the integrity of the eye, moving over chaos, but repudiating chaos by the fact of its attention. The mind, displayed in a tumble of sentences, was the world's organizing angel, the companion of a life. To notice was to follow faithfully. A faithful companion. *Whither thou goest, I will go.*

Every few months Sister Mary Louise handed me new sheet music. I never knew exactly when this would happen, but it always renewed my flagging, phony dedication to discipline. Getting new sheet music was turning over a literal new leaf. I hadn't mastered the earlier pieces, but Sister probably felt I'd gone as far as I was going to get, given my louche practice habits. New music might help. Her moist, protuberant eyes shone behind her glasses, radiating an unshakable trust in extending the second, third, and ever-renewable next chance.

The new music, often from European publishers, was crisp and fresh. Sister's favorites—and mine—came from France, the cream pages of Éditions A. Durand et fils, the publisher of Saint-Saëns and Debussy. Durand employed a sinuous art nouveau font on its covers, its address printed at the bottom left. The words *rue* and *Paris* attested to its exotic location, yet also to a real place you could go to if you ever somehow got yourself to Paris, unlikely as that was.

The paper was thin, so porous it attracted dirt and

smudges. The willowy pages were taller than stout American sheet music. I knew from experience, the paper would soon lose its starch. The pages would go limp on the music stand, soften at the edges, wrinkle and tear as I hauled them back and forth from home to school. Before long, the luscious cream paper would be shabby, the allure lost.

But I always forgot this on the day I received the new sheets. On new music days, today was always the first day of the rest of my life of good intentions. Today I was a believer. Perfection was very near. I could touch it.

A Saturday morning in May, therefore, and I had biked on my blue Raleigh three-speed to the convent and been admitted by Sister Portress to the strangely empty halls, so busy during the week, up the dark staircase to the fourth floor where Sister Mary Louise awaited me. The room was spacious, but like all music studios it felt cramped, two baby grands bulging their big hips at each other, a white bust of Chopin on one, a bloodless Schubert on the other.

The windows of the studio were tall, set so high the view was all sky and the ends of a few beseeching elm trees, freshly budded. The aerial view gave the odd sensation of being on a plane, though I had never been on a plane. No problem— mind travel in the practice room had provided the experience of flight long ago.

On windy days the big panes of glass rattled in their sashes. This early day in May was very windy, overcast, clouds bundling their way from window to window in a big troubled hurry, the windows clattering.

Today we begin again. This is how Sister Mary Louise

spoke on new music days. She too was a believer—what else?—she was a nun after all. She beamed at me. I was a good girl, and such a talker. I could make her laugh. I could surprise her just by saying how something struck me. When the rain hits the black asphalt of the street, I told her one day, it looks just like ballerinas on point. *How ever did you think of that?* she said in her mild, astonished way. Once I said I wished science would come up with a pill for breakfast, lunch, and dinner so a person wouldn't have to stop reading for meals—and of course there would be no dishes to do. She looked appalled, as if I had suggested something shameful. *Some of us look forward to our dinner,* she said, abashed, her plump self settled under the black tarp of her habit.

Today we begin again. She rose from her chair and went to the tall oak cupboard along the back wall where sheet music was neatly stacked on shelves in a system known only to her. She returned, holding the unblemished folder of Debussy's *La fille aux cheveux de lin* in the delicious Éditions Durand cream. The girl with the flaxen hair, one of the watery pieces she favored.

She sat at the other piano and played it straight through. The lilt of lyrical girlhood floated with aquatic ease from her capable hands over the light-and-dark waters of the Impressionists. She handed me the music. I opened the virgin sheets carefully while she reminded me that the metronome was my friend, and called out as usual, *Count, dear, count.* She reached over and made several marks on the music with her soft lead pencil to indicate the fingering she wanted me to follow, sometimes overruling the printed fingerings of Durand et fils.

I didn't like these pencil marks. They marred the page. But at the end of the lesson I closed the folder and placed the thin sheets carefully between my battered Bach *French Suites* and Schubert's sturdy *Moments Musicaux,* and everything was fine, though the flimsy Debussy extended beyond the heft of Bach and Schubert. But so what? The first day of the rest of my life of good intentions was before me, still perfect, a matter of unbroken imagining. Downstairs, I retrieved my bike, and rolled the music gently, positioning it in the wicker basket attached to the handlebars so nothing would be jammed or damaged.

I jumped on the bike, took the curb with a frisky leap at the corner of Fairmount and Grotto (the monastic names of those St. Paul streets!), and flew toward home, down the clickety-clack bumps of Fairmount's creosote paving. The streets still paved with these old blocks—only a few were left in the city—echoed with the memory of horse hooves when you rattled over them.

Have I ever been so happy for no good reason? A bolt of ecstasy shot through me. I was in New York—no, I was in Paree! On some rue just like Durand et fils. I rode a beam of invisible light straight to heaven—which (the five-year diary well knew) I didn't believe in anymore, but there it was, and I was in it.

The happiness arose from relief—I see that now. I hadn't been humiliated in the usual way by my lurching Bach, my careening Schubert. I hadn't had to face reality. Always a happy occasion. On new music days Sister did most of the playing. Nothing was expected of me. Now, on the bike, I skimmed madly downhill, demented with liberty. The girl with the flaxen hair was safe in the basket, my own brown hair blew in the wind. I considered trying to steer hands-free, which my brother said girls were no good at.

How brief the bliss, how long the memory.

A dark dash of rain, as if targeted, hit the moss-colored Schubert, leaving a forest green stain just as I reached the bottom of the hill. Then another, another, big jots splatting down lazily before the deluge, polka-dotting the sidewalk. I jumped off the bike at the corner of Victoria. Schubert could go, no problem sacrificing Bach.

But *La fille au cheveux de lin* must be saved. I couldn't leave the music in the basket and keep riding—Debussy's creamy edges peeked out from under Schubert's shabby over-coat like a delicate silk chemise.

I put the bike on the kickstand, grabbed the music, lifted my blouse, and stowed the bundle against my blessedly flat chest. And stood there, my arms crossed, the rain coming down now in earnest. Just stood there. I couldn't get on the bike—I needed both hands to hold the music in place. So my brother is right—girls are no good at riding hands-free.

Where to go? What to do? I was getting drenched. This rain was no ballerina on point. Furious sheets came down at a horizontal tilt. The music was sticking to my skin.

A car stopped, a man rolled down his window. *Why are you crying, little girl? Are you hurt?* I remember he said "little girl." I hadn't realized I was crying.

Never talk to strange men.

"*The Girl with the Flaxen Hair* is getting ruined," I sobbed across to him, maddened with misery, holding myself tightly around the chest, sniveling, snot out my nose. *Never call it snot, dear.*

His kindly smile faded. I was a crazy child.

Did I know where I lived?

"Of course I know where I live," I snapped at him. *Never give them your address.*

Gently, tentatively, he offered me a ride home—he could fit my bicycle in the back, he said.

Nothing doing, mister. *Never get in a stranger's car.*

"My new music's getting all ruined," I sobbed, furious at him for being available and yet not available, enraged at him for being a stranger.

If I would tell him where I lived, he said sensibly, he could deliver the music safely, and I could ride home on my bike. Would that be okay?

I stared at him. Decision time.

I hedged over to the car, fished the music out from under my shirt, thrust it in his window. The girl with the flaxen hair would have to go off with the stranger. I gave him our address.

Oh, that's just a few blocks away, he said. He smiled as if the problem were solved. He told me to ride home safely. *Stay on the sidewalks,* he said. *The creosote blocks get slippery in the rain.* A remark my father would make.

That's all.

Except for my mother's ferocity, the result of her heart-stopping terror when she'd looked out the window to see a stranger walking up the front stairs with my sheet music— the familiar Schubert and Bach. And no me. *I thought you'd been hit by a car. I thought you were dead.* She seemed exasperated that I wasn't.

Why on earth, she wanted to know, didn't I just keep riding home in the rain? I was so near. We could put the sheet music on the radiator to dry. No harm done. Everything would be fine. I was making a mountain out of a molehill. As usual.

Her sensible sigh. *Don't act like a sausage. It's nothing to cry over.*

But Mother, there's always something to cry over, to think over, muse over, fret and fume over. It's why, as Montaigne says, a person *meddles with writing.* Crying is only part of it, not even the important part, though the most theatrical. The little red book with the lock is getting an earful tonight.

The Debussy had absorbed a little of Schubert's green. Ruined. Nothing is perfect for long, though sometimes it's perfect for a little while. It can only be pried out of the moment, sequestered between the red leatherette covers where it begins its career as a memory. Bits of reality are pressed to the pages like wildflowers, flattened and faded, but *there.*

Perfect register between self and world—it does sometimes occur, fugitive, fleeting. There it was in the wicker basket on the handlebars of the Raleigh three-speed for its nanosecond. Worth noting.

The exquisite moment when the music flowed from Sister's fine old hands, and then my body braved the wind, the blond girl and I taking the turn deftly at Grotto, the horses of history clattering under the bicycle wheels. All of this in a mind full of future, revved with good intentions that would turn—I swear, *ma soeur!*—into good deeds. I will practice, I will give a perfect performance next Saturday.

Happiness can hold a lot of freight, and I was overloaded with joy that day, the hooves of the Raleigh clicking on Fairmount before the deluge.

It was nothing. Nothing to cry over. Nothing at all, really. But how many times has it floated me over despair? Just to think of that moment. The music and the speeding blue three-speed I commanded, hair whipped in the wind, the clattering old paving stones. I rolled this inner photograph gently, *molto pianissimo,* into the kit bag of consciousness. The ground beat of being, pounding like a heart, *forte, forte.*

"It is an absolute perfection and virtually divine to know how to enjoy our being rightfully," Montaigne says. He's thinking of the naked men his simple crude fellow has told him he saw in the New World. There's that touch of envy, maybe simply admiring wistfulness. To be so perfect in your being. To enjoy rightfully.

Utter joy is rare. Divine almost, he's saying. Of course it's a new world. It always is. This is the *essai* where, he insists, he would strip naked to display his entire self, if only writing could do that. It is the purpose of such work, its glory, its task.

You and I talked about this, sitting at the yellow table in

the kitchen. You said it was poetry, this quality of attention. *Poetry comes first,* you said. Now I wonder—why didn't I ask as we sat there?—did you mean it comes first in human history, the cry antedates the story? Or were you claiming poetry is the greater thing?

I should have asked. But I do remember that whenever I asked you to judge—as I so often did—which is better, this or that, which is your favorite or the best, you smiled (or frowned) and said, *Why do you always have to judge things? Why can't you love both, let it go at that?*

I couldn't help insisting, nagging you for choices you refused to make, hierarchies you wouldn't construct in the face of life's contradictory richness. We loved to talk about language, trading slang and habits of speaking. The Minnesota passive Scandinavian conditional, as you called it: *How old a man would he be?* This slithery locution instead of frankly asking, *How old is he?*

Toward the end you gloried in listening to kids say *Whatever,* pronounced with exquisite teen dismissiveness, *Whatever,* when responding to an ethical dilemma or a parental urgency. *What-ever,* you said to me the last week, an old man mimicking perfectly a kid without a care, smiling with all the time in the world. What talkers we were in that kitchen, the coffee getting cold between us.

We met on this, at least, our trust that the moment lies somewhere ahead—not far—when, surely, everything can be said. Perfect register between the instrument of self and the mysterious machine of the world. You listened to me on this point, nodded. Didn't tease, didn't say *What-ever.*

You got it, what I was thinking. How a person has to stand in the rain, protect the girl with the flaxen hair, the fierce, fragile lyrical self. Not to hide her, not to control her. Just to keep in reserve the alert intimacy of that ardent heart. There's waiting to do, always. Big part of the job—waiting.

Montaigne called what he was doing "meddling with writing," as if it were impossible simply to latch onto a subject, *write* it for God's sake, and be done with it. He discovered that the act of writing gets all tangled up in what is supposed to be "the subject." Writing *becomes* the subject, or becomes part of the subject. Meddling. Maybe a vexed word for *describing,* for going round and round the "subject" until it becomes the writing. Or the other way around—the writing becomes the subject.

I was coming down the last lap of my last book, a memoir full of people dying and finally dead—Mother, Dad. You were not far behind (though I managed to pretend that wasn't so). We were both good at pretending. You were alive in that book full of their deaths. I was painfully aware of just how specific every bit of writing is, full of choices and chances, not theoretical at all, not the business of sweeping statements or smart ideas about "form" or "genre" or anything remotely theoretical. Just subject-verb-object and the hope of meaning.

Two nights away from the finish of my book, I was working late. I looked away from the computer screen for a moment and there was the dog staring at me. She was on the verge of speech. I could see it. *Come to bed.* Her eyes said this clearly. It was almost 2 a.m. and for the past four hours I've been changing commas to dashes and then back again to commas with the fixation only a fanatic can sustain.

"You've become a crazy person again," I said right out loud. The dog padded away.

J. F. Powers was once asked by a colleague in the corridor at their university how things were going. Powers allowed that it had been a tough day—"I spent the morning trying to decide whether to have my character call his friend *pal* or *chum*," he said.

That's what it often comes to—thinking how important the choice of *pal* or *chum* is, how whatever truth writing lays claim to resides in a passion for just such mad micro-distinctions. This monomania is what a novelist friend calls the six-hundred-pound gorilla of a book. Once the six-hundred-pound gorilla gets hold of you, you're his (or hers). "Those last weeks of finishing a book are a world in themselves," she said. "I think that gorilla is the reason most of us write—it's a real high, but it's also a subconscious agreement not to be available or even normal for as long as it takes."

Montaigne was an obsessive reviser. Or not a reviser so much as an adder-on, an expander. Same with Whitman.

Both of them were writers who wrote one book: themselves. *Who holds this holds a man* (Whitman), and *I am myself the matter of my book* (Montaigne).

But as soon as you break away from the gorilla's embrace of a particular book, those big, rangy questions begin to make their approach again. Maybe this is especially true of memoir, the odd enterprise of "writing a life" that has captivated our literary life for the last two decades or so. We tend to think of the novel as the classic narrative form—ever evolving, but familiar, its stately provenance long the preserve of academic interest and the center of trade publishing. Whereas the memoir seems new or somehow "modern," a rather suspect literary upstart. And therefore a form that invites interrogation.

But strictly speaking, autobiography is a genre far older than the novel, and is hardwired into Western literary history. Perhaps from that first injunction of the oracle at Delphi—*Know thyself*—Western culture has been devoted to the exploration of individual consciousness and the unspooling of the individual life.

That commandment to *know thyself* was central to antiquity. Plato uttered a version of it; Cicero used it in a tract on the development of social concord. It was such a pillar of cultural, even spiritual value that in the early Christian period Clement of Alexandria felt compelled to claim that the saying had been borrowed by the Greeks from scripture, thus binding the two developing spiritualities—pagan and monotheistic—together in a seamless endeavor.

Closer to modernity, Goethe is supposed to have said with

a shudder, "Know thyself? If I knew myself, I'd run away." André Gide probably expressed this revulsion best: "Know thyself! A maxim as pernicious as it is ugly. Whoever observes himself arrests his own development. A caterpillar who wanted to know itself well would never become a butterfly."

But the strongest indictment I've encountered came from a student in Indiana who had been conscripted by his Freshman Comp teacher to attend a reading I gave some years ago. He sprawled in his chair with his baseball cap on backwards (always a bad sign), his eloquent body language making it clear he was far, far away. A very *What-ever* person. Can't win 'em all, I thought, and carried on, my eye straying back to him like a tongue drawn to the absence of a just-pulled tooth.

During the Q&A I fielded the decorous questions the students posed. And then, suddenly, apparently in response to something I'd said, my antihero sat bolt upright, and was waving his hand urgently, his face alight with interest. Ah—a convert. I called on him, smiling.

"I get it," he said. "Nothin's ever happened to you—and you write books about it."

In pronouncing this acute critical remark, he touched on the most peculiar aspect of the rise of the memoir—or perhaps the personal essay, the miniature form that relies in our age on autobiography—namely, that fundamentally it isn't about having a more interesting life than someone else. True, there is a strand of autobiographical writing that relies on the documentation of extraordinary circumstances, lives lived in extremity, often at great peril. But such memoirs have always been part of the record, and of literary history. What characterizes the rise of memoir in recent times is precisely the opposite condition—not a gripping "narrative arc," but the quality of voice, the story of perception rather than action.

The self is not the subject in this kind of book, but its instrument. And the work of the self is not to "narrate" but to describe. There is something fundamentally photographic about memoir, photographic rather than cinematic. Not a story, but a series of tableaux we are given to consider. No memoirist is surprised by the absences and blanks in action, for another unavoidable quality of autographical writing as I am thinking of it—as lyrical quest literature—is that it is as much about reticence as it is about revelation.

It is often remarked that the advent of the movies and the ever-faster pace of modern life have conspired to make description a less essential part of prose narrative in our times. We don't need to be told what things look like—we are inundated with images, pictures, moving or static. In this view, we need the opposite of the photographic quality so beloved of nineteenth-century descriptive writing in which the landscape is rolled out, sentence after sentence, the interior of a room and the interior of the character's mind meticulously presented, paralleling each other.

We require writing, instead, that subsumes description, leaps right over it to frame episode and to create the much-sought-after narrative arc. The motto—even the mantra—of this narrative model is of course the commandment of introductory fiction-writing workshops: *Show, don't tell.*

But as recent memoir writing shows, descriptive writing abounds. And it proves, finally, not to be about the object described. Or not only. Description in memoir is where the consciousness of the writer and the material of the story are established in harmony, where the self is lost in the material, in a sense. In fiction of the show-don't-tell variety narrative scenes that "show" and dutifully do not "tell" are advanced by volleys of dialogue in which the author's presence is successfully obscured by the dramatic action of the dialogue of his characters. But in description we hear and feel the absorption of the author in the material. We sense the presence of the creator of the scene.

This personal absorption is what we mean by "style." It's strange that we would choose so oddly surfacey a word—style—for this most soulful aspect of writing. We could more exactly call this relation between consciousness and its subject "integrity." What else is the articulation of personal perception?

Style is a word usually claimed by fashion and the most passing aesthetic values. But maybe that's as it should be, because style in writing is terribly perishable. It can rot—that is what we mean when we recognize writing to be "precious," for example. But at its best, style is the register between a writer's consciousness and the material being wrestled to the page. It is the real authority of a writer, more substantial than plot, less ego-dependent than voice.

In 1951, Alfred Kazin published his memoir of his boyhood in Brooklyn, *A Walker in the City,* the book that established the modern American memoir. Leslie Fiedler admired the book, but was also frustrated by it. It "perversely refuses to be a novel," he said with some annoyance, as if Kazin's book, deeply dependent on descriptive writing, were refusing to behave. And it was.

I was one of those enthralled teenage readers of long nineteenth-century English novels. I toiled my way through dense descriptions of gloomy heaths and bogs to get to the airy volleys of dialogue that lofted back and forth down the page to give me what I wanted. Would Jane and Mr. Rochester . . . or would they not? Would Dorothea Brooke awaken— would Mr. Lydgate? I didn't relish the descriptive passages. I endured them. Just as Jane and Dorothea endured their parched lives, as if these endless descriptive passages were the desert to be crossed before the paradise of dialogue and the love story could be entered.

Yet all this description was, after all, the *world* of the book—not simply because it gave the book a "sense of place," as the old literary chestnut puts it. It wasn't a "sense of place" I cared about, but the meeting place of perception with story—the place where someone *claimed* the story, where I could glimpse the individual consciousness, the creator of the scene. The person pulling the wires and making Jane and Dorothea move. I was looking, I suppose, for a sign of intimacy with the invisible author. That "dear reader" moment so familiar to nineteenth-century novels. Think of Thackeray pausing to have a chat with the reader—with me!—about how to live on nothing a year. Or George Eliot breaking off to describe the furnishings of Dorothea's ardent mind.

Henry James, crown prince of nineteenth-century describers, flaneur of the sentence, lounge lizard of the paragraph, takes his own sweet time to unfurl an observation, smoking the cheroot of his thought in the contemplative after-dinner puffery of a man who knows how to draw out the pleasure of his rare tobacco. Or—because James himself never hesitates to pile up opposing figures of speech until he has sliced his thought to the refracted transparency he requires—why not just switch metaphors and say that James sits mildly at his torture apparatus, turning the crank in meticulously calibrated movements as the reader lies helplessly strained upon the rack of his ever-expanding sentences, the exquisite pain of the lengthening description almost breaking the bones of attention. In short (as James often says after gassing on for a nice fat paragraph or two on the quality of a Venetian sunset or the knowing lift of a European eyebrow glimpsed across a table by an artless American ingénue), in short, he loves to carry on.

Carrying on, I was discovering, is what it is to describe. A lot. At length. To trust description above plot, past character development, and even theme. To understand that to describe is both humbler and more essential than to think of compositional imponderables such as "voice" or to strain toward superstructures like "narrative arc." To trust that the act of description will *find* voice and out of its streaming attention will take hold of narration.

By the time I was considering all of this, I had passed from being a reader and had become the more desperate literary type—a writer trying to figure out how to do it. I was practicing without a license, never having taken a prose-writing course. I had no idea how to "sustain a narrative," and didn't even understand at the time (1980) that I was writing something called a "memoir." Yet when I read *Speak, Memory,* and later read Nabokov's command—*Caress the detail, the divine detail*—I knew I had found the motto I could live by, the one that prevailed over "show, don't tell."

Perhaps only someone as thoroughly divested of his paradise as Nabokov had been of his boyhood Russia, his native language, and all his beloved associations and privileged expectations could enshrine the detail, the fragment, as the god of his literary religion, could trust the truths to be found in the DNA of detail, attentively rendered in ardent description. The dutiful observation that is the yeoman's work of description finally ascended, Nabokov demonstrated, to the transcendent reality of literature—to metaphor.

Nabokov was asked in an interview if his characters ever "took over." He replied icily that *his* characters were his galley slaves.

Yet when it was a matter of locating the godhead of literary endeavor, even a writer as imperious as Nabokov did not point to himself and his powers but to the lowly detail. *Caress the detail, the divine detail.* Next to grand conceptions like plot, which is the legitimate government of most stories, or character, which is the crowned sovereign, the detail looks like a ragged peasant with a half-baked idea of revolution and a crazy, sure glint in its eye. But here resides divinity. Henry

James emerges again with his faith in "the rich principle of the Note."

In attending to the details, in the act of description, the more dynamic aspects of narrative have a chance to reveal themselves—not as "action" or "conflict" or any of the theoretical and technical terms we persist in thinking of as the sources of form. Rather, description gives the mind a place to *be* in relation with the reality of the world.

It was a desire for the world's memoir—history—that, paradoxically, drew me to memoir, that seemingly personal form. I wanted to understand—or at least touch—the oppositions of the Cold War that had formed me. My Czech grandmother, a stray foreign figment from "the old country," living with us in what I grew up calling the free world. Yet the great world—the place I wanted to find—could not possibly be in Minnesota. You had to get out on the road to find it, let it rough you up. Another reason Montaigne appealed: a man who said he was most at home on his horse, riding free across unknown terrain, but who comes to us as the man sequestered in his tower, alone with words. The personal and the historical, twisted together. So that old motto of my Sixties Generation youth—the personal is political—wasn't true after all. The personal isn't political, it's historical. A rangier, yet more intimate embrace of oppositions, as the Cold War was a neat polar division for decades, the prevailing myth of most of my life.

These oppositions meant that as a writer I tended toward description, not to narrative, not to story. Maybe the root of the impulse to write is always lost—properly lost—in the nonliterary earth of what we call real life. And craft, as we think of it, is just the jargon we give to that darker, earthier medium.

It was my mother who was the storyteller in our house. I was her audience. Her dear reader, in a way. I simply—sometimes bitterly—understood that nothing much was happening in our modest midwestern lives, yet I clung to the drama with which she infused every vignette, every encounter at the grocery store. Nothing came of it all, but still, the details as she cast them before me were enthralling. Our nothing life sparkled with words. With description.

And when I sought to make sense of the world that kept slipping away to the past, to loss and forgetfulness, when I protested inwardly at that disappearance, it was to description I instinctively turned. Coming from a first love of poetry and therefore being a literalist, it didn't occur to me to copy other prose writers. If I wanted to learn to write descriptively, I needed—what else?—pictures.

I took myself off to the Minneapolis Institute of Art and sat down in front of a Bonnard. I wrote the painting. Described it. I went home and looked at a teacup on the table—wrote that too. Still-life descriptions that ran on for several pages. I wrote and wrote, describing my way through art galleries and the inadvertent still lifes of my house and my memory, my grandmother's garden, her Sunday dinners.

To my growing astonishment, these descriptive passages, sometimes running two, three pages, even longer, had a way of shearing off into narrative after all. The teacup had been given to me by my mother. And once I thought of the fact that she had bought these cups, made in Czechoslovakia, as a bride just before the Second World War, I was writing about that war, about my mother and her later disappointments, which somehow were—and were not—part of this fragile cup. Description, which had seemed like background in novels, static and inert as a butterfly pinned to the page of my notebook, proved to be a dynamic engine that stoked voice and, even more, propelled the occasional narrative arc.

Written from the personal voice of my own perception, description proved even to be the link with the world's story, with history itself. Here was my mother's teacup, made in Czechoslovakia before the war, and here, therefore, was not only my mother's heartbreak, but Europe's. The detail was surely divine, offering up miracles of connections out of the faithful consideration of the fragments before me. No wonder Nabokov was a passionate butterfly hunter—more bright details pinned to a board.

We sense this historical power at the heart of autobiographical writing in the testaments from the Holocaust, from the Gulag, from every marginal and abused life that has spoken its truth, which is often its horror, to preserve its demonic details—and in so doing has seen them become divine.

The history of whole countries, of an entire era and even lost populations, depends sometimes on a little girl faithfully keeping her diary. The great contract of literature consists in this: you tell me your story and somehow I get my story. If we are looking for another reason to explain the strangely powerful grip of the first-person voice on contemporary writing, perhaps we need look no further than the power of Anne Frank's equation: that to write one's life enables the world to preserve and, more, to comprehend its history.

But what of lives lived in the flyover? Lives that don't have that powerful, if terrible, historical resonance of radical suffering. Ordinary lives. Mine in middling Minnesota in the middle of the twentieth century. Why bother to describe it? Because all details are divine, not just Nabokov's. In fact, the poorer the supposed value, the more the detail requires description to attest to its divinity.

Which brings me to—if not a story, yet another vignette. Early in my teaching life, I went (foolishly) through a killer Minnesota snowstorm to get to the university because I had student conferences scheduled. You tried to dissuade me, but there was no stopping me (*you can count on me*). The university had closed by the time I arrived. The campus was empty, whipped by white shrouds of blizzard snow, the wind whistling down the mall. I sat in my office in the empty building, cursing my ruinous work ethic, wondering if the buses would keep running so I could get home. *Don't go,* you'd said that morning. *I'll worry about you. Don't go.* Surely you knew any attempt to "control" me—my word, not yours—only ratified any scheme or plan I had in mind.

Then a rap on my office door. I opened it and there, like an extra out of *Dr. Zhivago,* stood my eleven o'clock, a quiet sophomore, Tommy.

He looked anxious. He was really glad I was there, he said, because he had a big problem with the assignment. I had asked the students to write short autobiographies. "I just can't

write anything about my life," he said, head down, boots pud-
dling on the floor.

I waited for the disclosure. What would it be—child
abuse, incest? What murder or mayhem could this boy not
divulge? What had brought him trooping through the blizzard
to get help with his life story? How would I get him to Student Counseling? Was Student Counseling even open?

"What's the problem?" I asked, not wanting to know, but
adopting what I hoped was a neutral therapeutic tone.

"See," he said miserably, "I come from Fridley," naming
one of the nowhere suburbs sprawling drearily beyond the
freeway north of Minneapolis.

I stared at him. I didn't, for a moment, comprehend that
this was the dark disclosure, this the occasion of his misery:
being from Fridley meant, surely, that he had nothing to say.
In effect, had no life.

There it was again—nothin' had ever happened to him
and I was asking him to write about it.

"I have good news for you, Tommy," I said. "The field's
wide open—nobody has told what it's like to grow up in Fridley yet. It's all yours."

Wasn't this Montaigne's problem—and he a *seigneur, un
grand homme*—setting himself the assignment to sit in his
cold tower and say what he saw, what he thought, professing
in his "To the Reader" note, the half page that precedes the
Essais, that "you would be unreasonable to spend your leisure
on so frivolous and vain a subject." Even Montaigne felt compelled, though nothing had happened to him, to write books
about it.

Sit there and describe. And because the detail is divine, if you caress it into life, the world lost or ignored, the world ruined or devalued, comes to life. The little world you alone can bring into being, bit by broken bit, angles into the great world. It's voice, your style. Or, call it what it is—your integrity.

When you come upon the statue of Montaigne in Paris, you find him amid overgrown greenery in the Carré Paul-Painlevé, across from the main approach to the Sorbonne on the rue des Écoles. He's sequestered in the bushes, as if in bronze he preferred the margin he chose in life. The first thing you notice is his shoe. Even at night, the shoe emerges clearly, golden against the dusky bronze of his casually seated figure, cross-legged, bending forward as if to catch what you might be saying there on the sidewalk.

People rub the shoe for luck or maybe out of affection. A shoe-rub is said to assure a good exam result across the street. It glows from all this human touch, an elegant sixteenth-century Mary Jane dancing slipper, blushing from generations of twentieth-century fondling. The sculptor, Paul Landowski, is better known for his gigantic 1931 Flash Gordon statue of Christ the Redeemer overlooking Rio de Janeiro, an art deco Jesus. Montaigne's statue was done two years later, in 1933, perhaps to honor the four hundredth anniversary of his birth in 1533.

Something of the dandy about that shoe. Then the face, surprisingly intent, looking back at you. The face of a man who appreciates the finer things, wryly amused by this weakness for pleasure, not haunted by his appetites. Landowski has given Montaigne a twentieth-century face, nonchalant, warm, easy—a winning American midcentury face.

This bronze Montaigne, like the one I've been reading these recent years, sees it all and accepts it all in advance—the "all" of human perversity and contradiction and marvel played out on the field of avidity and longing. With abundant relish and genial curiosity, he would take easily to the shapeshifting of our times. Gay/straight? Transgender? Intersex? He was pondering versions of these possibilities in an early essay from 1572, "Of the Power of the Imagination," piling up examples ("a man whom the Bishop of Soissons had named Germain at confirmation, but whom all the inhabitants of the place had seen and known as a girl named Marie until the age of twenty-two. He was now heavily bearded."). Without dismay, he regarded this richness of possibility as evidence of the natural state of human affairs, an aspect of the legitimate sovereignty of the imagination and, thus, imagination the best judge of reality: "It is not so great a marvel that this sort of accident is frequently met with"—his laconic response to the array of identities. This is, after all, the man who said of his work that he didn't portray being—"I portray passing." Ripeness is *not* all. Change is. Flux as the only genuine constant. Life not as a circle but a spinning spiral, the imagination running the show.

There it is again at the heart of life—the imagination, that old *occasion of sin* under the beechnut tree, leaves swishing above, body flat on planet earth, the mind aloft, refusing to behave, even if I was (and I was) a good girl, and also now, all these years later, as I was told in Llangollen, a nice lady.

The imagination as the crucible of freedom. We are made to contend with life along that ragged seam of being. Consciousness, Montaigne is saying, will accommodate just about anything. It is our rightful business to think, to muse, to wonder—to describe—using this image-beset faculty of mind for the job. One vignette after another.

Montaigne was perfectly positioned to display the power of the imagination, perched at the pivot of medieval magic, angling toward modern rationalism. "To me, magicians are poor authorities," he says. "Nevertheless . . ." And on he goes to list charms and weirdnesses he's heard of or witnessed himself that attest to the sovereignty of the imagination—flying monks, various "fabulous testimonies," and a homely vignette of his own, his observation as exact as a lab researcher taking notes:

> Recently at my house a cat was seen watching a bird on a treetop, and, after they had locked gazes for some time, the bird let itself fall as if dead between the cat's paws, either intoxicated by its own imagination or drawn by some attracting power of the cat.

Montaigne is a great believer in thinking-makes-it-so, and tells of a woman who was informed, as a prank, that she was eating a pie made of cat meat. She believed—or too completely imagined—what she was told, seeing in horrified detail the kitty she had just scarfed down. She "fell into a violent stomach disorder and fever." The result of this overactive imagination? "It was impossible to save her." There's the imagination for you.

It was raining the night I first saw the Montaigne statue, and though it may seem I was seeking another of my literary shrines, in fact we—yes, you were on this trip too—we just happened upon it. We were running late, trying to locate a fish restaurant recommended by a friend who knows Paris. Dripping in his leafy bower by the university, gleaming from the wet—or maybe because I'd been reading him, living with his sinuous sentences in my head, and had no idea such a statue existed—this bronze Montaigne had something of the apparition about him. Like Whitman, another eccentric of the first-person voice, he was just loafing by the side of the road.

Out with the iPhone. Snap snap. Got the shoe. Didn't, couldn't quite, get the face.

You were patient, standing there in the dripping cold, holding the black umbrella over me as I got the shoe, tried for the face. Only now I see you were glad to pause in the rain, glad not to keep up the pace. It was the beginning of slowing down, the beginning of your *bum ticker* deciding things, the beat slowing, slower. Stopped, finally. But we didn't think that then—or I didn't. I thought you were being patient, something I could never be accused of—rushing, always rushing.

Take as long as you need, you said. The beginning of slowness. Or the beginning of patience. These things creep up on a life, in the dark, in the rain. In our case, with the genial bronze man smiling indulgently from the hedgerow.

For Montaigne it starts with death, his "meddling with writing." Death occasions his decision to retire from his life as a courtier, a public life, to his cold tower, in order to see how he sees things (which is to say how he describes things).

In swift remove, he lost his admired father, Pierre, five infant daughters, and a brother, absurdly, from a tennis ball to the head (sixteenth-century tennis balls were made of wood, which does take the bounce out of the game). All of these relations were gone before or soon after he retired to his château in Périgord. He was thirty-eight.

But the searing, permanent heartbreak was the early death of his beloved friend Étienne de La Boétie, the great love of his life. He would have understood the Ladies: his great love was a friendship, not a liaison, though our age of course suggests he was "really" gay—probably, potentially, maybe, surely . . . Maybe he was, maybe he would have been. But he saw the relationship—and mourned it—as the perfect friendship, and he saw friendship as the perfect relation. Marriage he treats with a kind of measured contempt, a wearisome necessity (*Marriage can be compared to a cage: birds outside it despair to enter, and birds within, to escape*), his own wife (with whom he had six daughters) an afterthought. And his mother, barely mentioned, while his father was adored.

It was the loss of the perfect friend he mourned, a loss that never would, never could be comforted. Such a friend could never be replaced—except perhaps by continuing the magical intercourse of shared thought by writing what amounted to letters, the *Essais*. "It was a melancholy humor, and consequently a humor very hostile to my natural disposition, produced by the gloom of solitude into which I had cast myself some years ago, that first put into my head this day-dream of meddling with writing," he says. Donald M. Frame, Montaigne's great biographer and translator, believes that if La Boétie had lived—no essays. Even Montaigne believed that if he had "a strong friend to address," he would have been "more successful" as a letter writer. In effect, we're reading in the *Essais* something between a diary and a collection of letters—in any case, personal documents.

At the Paris fish restaurant, which we finally located, you were making a pitch for a different trip—to Sweden—for Linnaeus, that eighteenth-century figure you kept encouraging me to pursue, the Swedish botanist whose system of binomial nomenclature (like the Ladies, he was a System person) earned him the title "father of modern taxonomy." Surely a botanist was another daydreamer, a leisure man? A lot of peacefulness in botany. Think about it.

I did. I liked this idea partly because my father, a romantic florist who rolled off the Latin binomial names of plants in the greenhouse, always tried to get the rest of us to do the same. Daisy? Why not have the pleasure of saying *Bellis perennis?* A rose is a rose is a rose, of course. But the daffodil? Let it luxuriate in its full Linnaean title—*Narcissus sylvestris.*

Rousseau, who had no time for Montaigne, asked a friend to send a message to Linnaeus on his behalf: "Tell him I know no greater man on earth."

Goethe piled on about his brilliance as well: "With the exception of Shakespeare and Spinoza," he wrote breathlessly, "I know no one among the no longer living who has influenced me more strongly!"

It was an opinion Linnaeus shared: "No one," he wrote of himself, "has been a greater Botanicus or Zoologist. No one has written more books, more correctly, more methodically, from his own experience. No one has more completely changed a whole science and initiated a new epoch. No one has become more of a household name throughout the world." He also modeled for the new epoch the essential modern quality—a gift for public relations based on self-regard.

Still, the idealization of the *new epoch* was perhaps the key to the praise others lavished on him. The idea of finding a *system*—or not finding one but constructing one—for all of creation was at the beating heart of the Enlightenment's dawning romance with science. How thrilling not to be lost forever in wonder, that ancient veil cast over life's mysteries. How amazing to discern a relation for it all, the connective tissue of creation.

Linnaeus's *Systema Naturae* and *Species Plantarum* formed a classification system, housekeeping for observed forms (zoological and botanical). That the system was not a key to internal structures and didn't anticipate evolution (Linnaeus saw creation as static—his goal was to describe "what God had created" without the notion that this creation was an ongoing project—no "portraying passing" for him) did not stop his contemporaries from seeing his system as the work of genius.

Biology has augmented and complicated the understanding of living organisms since his time, but Linnaeus's naming system is still used today, slotting life in hierarchical order: domain, kingdom, phylum, class, order, family, genus, and species, the last two categories, genus and species, giving us the name and family relation of a particular plant.

Perhaps the great appeal—almost a sigh of relief from admirers like Goethe and Rousseau—came from the sense that Linnaeus was promoting science as a humane system, creating a universal language, and therefore making peace between science and philosophy (what we call "the humanities"). His taxonomy was not held tightfisted by gatekeeper specialists. The sexual identification system Linnaeus devised (based on number, size, and method of insertion of plant stamens and the female pistils) was open to anyone to use. Nor was it regional and limited. It was wondrously global in its reach.

But the more I read about Linnaeus himself—the grandiosity, the marshaling of his ranks of students (whom he preferred to call "apostles") in quasi-military uniforms, marching through Uppsala like a private militia, his mock Laplander costumes—the more I was drawn back to my modest monk and his pea plants in the Brno monastery garden. The garden was still my idea of Eden, the demilitarized zone of science where poetry—singing the Psalms—punctuated the lab work. I'm sorry—though you thought I should go there, and I said I would, I never went, after all, to Sweden. One of the things you never knew.

A fter all the shilly-shallying, the notetaking and reading, going here, going there, Montaigne plugged into my ear from the iPhone, before I was ready (or deserved?) to visit his . . . *world,* as I'd come to think of his tower, here it finally is, late April, and I'm driving with my English friend Annette in the passenger seat of the little rental car out of Charles de Gaulle, off at last to the château near Bordeaux.

If two people are still friends after negotiating the Périphérique out of Paris during rush hour, one hunched over the wheel, the other bent to the autoroute map to get the direction—*Left, left . . . no, straight!*—this is a friendship for the ages. And no, we did not have Google Maps or cell phone apps to lead the way. We were cast upon the torrential waves of the superhighway until finally we were funneled out of the traffic tsunami, from one slightly saner road to another and still another one yet more untraveled until at last, already at dusk, we were on something marked with the mild brown signs indicating a scenic or cultural heritage road, narrow, tree-lined, becalmed.

More than that—French. French as Sister Peronne Marie had taught us, the France of order and sane *plaisir*, three-hour lunches, the promise of wine and lavender and figs even if all that was a season in the future. It was blossom time, the landscape radiating youthful relish for the day, the meal, the moment.

The road was not called the route de Montaigne, but was named for the greater personage of Périgord: the goose. The Route du Foie Gras—in some English-language guides the Route of the Fatty Liver, suggesting a disgruntled vegetarian in charge of translation.

We didn't make a beeline for Montaigne's château. We seemed to be following his own meandering habits, content to get there a day later, make that two or three days later. *What-ever*. Or maybe we were fattening up on the spring glory of the region, like geese at their feed hoses, stopping our first night at an old château. Do I even know what, exactly, makes a building a château? It may have been just a rangy country house, not exactly tatty, but pleasantly worn around the edges. Nothing grand, but pleasantly ample. The place, we discovered, was often rented by local families for weddings, but this was a weekday and we had it to ourselves. The owners or perhaps the employees, almost off duty, cheerful and unrushed, hung around our table to talk—Annette really speaking French to them, I the patois I carried forward from high school.

We sat in the shadowy dining room overlooking a field

where horses occasionally passed by, heads down as if taken up with private considerations. A sideboard with dull silver plate, candelabras, a large chipped faience bowl mounded with green grapes, a few scissored leaves attached. Wine—of course, faded gold in cloudy goblets. Not Vlasta's severe Moser cut glass, her mother's fine crystal that had made its way through wars and the breakup of empire to sit in unlikely splendor on her *panalak* table. These were homey, frank *vin ordinaire* glasses, the rims rounded, the stems stout. Country glasses. We were offered more wine. Annette, using the delectable French idiom, nodded, smiled—*Une larme, s'il vous plaît.* Just a teardrop, please. But of course the glasses were filled to the top, the gold winking, night now covering the view.

A slightly mad quality attended the place, where the old was still alive, still dying right in front of you—the banged-up candlesticks dating from who knows when, cheek by jowl with a plastic-sheeted portrait of Marilyn Monroe fixed to a back wall, right against the good bones of the stone. Candles, the rest of the wine, chicken unctuous in a bronzed sauce, pale shallots pillowed under the soft lacquer of the sauce, and sweet. Then some kind of nut liqueur in tiny shot glasses. Sipping, sighing. The first night.

We stayed at other inns, some quite proud of themselves, one outfitted with an infinity pool, another with a stiffly tended garden, koi moving with exquisite idleness in the central lily pond. I still get email offers from one place, promising *un bon séjour,* urging Christmas, New Year's, perhaps my birthday? But that first night in the drafty old country house we found almost by mistake, and we the only guests, the shadowy rooms waiting, like backstage sets, to be brought forward for next weekend's wedding party, the off-duty horses unbridled till later in the week when they would be latched to the rickety bridal carriage—this was the sweetest place we stayed, the one that hasn't faded away. Strange that the name is nowhere to be found in my notebook. As if it never really existed, concocted sheerly of desire and the frenzied exhaustion of getting off the Périphérique and onto a roadway dedicated to the silken livers of snowy geese. (*They are happy—happy, madam— to be fed. Do not call it forced! They line up for the hose, they cannot wait!*)

This rather frazzled place is the one lodged in memory, though I have iPhone photos of the others, their color-coordinated lavender bedchambers, tender walls painted a rainy green, rouged-up interiors, fey settees with toile upholstery, and giant beribboned bundles of dried lavender in purple glass vases, design reminders that we were settled into a gentrified *France profonde*. But the pictures that persist are not on the iPhone but in the mind—that first night, the benign scruffiness of that nameless farmstead.

This preference was not simply occasioned by the hominess of the whole enterprise. Or if it was just that, I took the hominess as an assurance that we weren't being invited to congratulate ourselves on having located the upscale nostalgia of the restored and improved French country houses in the Luberon, farther south, of Peter Mayles and those who followed his well-polished dream in the 1990s real estate fever for *le sud*, a possessive love that changed forever the ancient habits of farm and pasture to gastrotourism. (Or saved it from the decay it had already entered? Depends on your source. As someone said, a developer is someone who wants to ruin a beloved landscape with a house; a preservationist is someone who already has a house there.)

We could feel that first night—a different kind of vanity— that we had dropped off the pleasure trail of the Route du Foie Gras and tumbled into the France beloved of the writers who had "discovered" it before it was massively discovered and deeply touristed—Ford Madox Ford and Sybille Bedford, and later, after the war, the American poets. W. S. Merwin, who owned a little ruined patch of Provence as a young man who fell in love with the Troubadour poets. And my first favorite—James Wright with his poems about Minnesota and then the ones about Nîmes, the world of snowfields (my world) leading him to the improbable fields of lavender and thyme. And here I was in it too. Finally and for real. Well, not for real. But for a time. Maybe an ardent note-taker, but still, I was a tourist.

I'd always imagined living in France. You teased me—no matter where we went, I was always checking real estate listings online, especially places in France. *We could sell the house, we could move to France! Yes, I suppose,* you would say, not rising to the bait. Sometimes when I got too annoying, you allowed yourself to say, *I thought you liked it here. I do,* I'd say, *I do, but . . .*

Once there was Google and Zillow, I was a lost cause. *Find any châteaus for us?* you'd ask, passing by my desk, the computer leaping from the Bouches-du-Rhône to Brittany, farmhouse to sea cottage. My expat life became a pure act of the imagination.

I wasn't thinking of Montaigne that first night on the way to his tower so much as of the life not lived—maybe only a midwesterner can sustain this geographic passion over a lifetime, the desire to be Elsewhere, even in the midst of a happy life. Our life. Tommy came to mind, the undergrad tromping through a Minnesota blizzard to confess forlornly that he had no life—he came from Fridley. That deepest midwestern sense of place, the yearning to escape. The homeboy Scott Fitzgerald got himself gone—and glad of it. Another of my literary heroes, Mavis Gallant. She abandoned the North American middle for the lonely loveliness of France. Think of her great expat stories. But she belonged to an earlier generation. The sorry hotels of her strays were out of a France W. S. Merwin and James Wright might have glimpsed, but that aura was more foreign to me even than the Provençal landscape.

In my reading, I sought a contemporary, someone who lived what I thought of as my "other life," the one not lived, but so lavishly imagined and desired that it felt not like another life, but a version of my own. You feel—I did—deep contentment when you find such a life expressed by a writer who has lived it, as if in reading that life you (sort of) live it too. Even better, if the writer is someone you have "discovered," the way people think they discover a landscape—this long-beloved landscape of France, for example.

Just before I came to France to visit Montaigne's tower, I found in a bookstore by accident just such a figure—Gustaf Sobin, born in 1935, so not my generation, but nearer than

Mavis Gallant, nearer than W. S. Merwin or James Wright. I didn't know anyone who had read him. Good. My find.

You, though, with your deep reach in American poetry, especially the experimental edges—friend of Ginsberg, promoter of Thom Gunn and Robert Creeley, encourager of Ed Sanders and the Fugs—you maybe had heard of Sobin. Possible. But you weren't talking, not anymore. Just me, still muttering around the house to you, the dog looking at me steadfastly, worried.

In spite of the intriguing continental name, Gustaf Sobin, I found, was an American. After graduation from Brown (he was born in Boston, had a private school education), he made the leap to France, looking for poetry. And found it in his hero (eventually his mentor and friend) René Char. Sobin arrived in Paris in 1962. He lived most of the rest of his life in the Vaucluse department of Provence, almost Montaigne country (given that Montaigne went to school in Toulouse). Sobin met and married a British painter there, and they had two children. He was already dead—from pancreatic cancer in 2005, just sixty-nine years old—when I discovered his books.

According to an online tourist site for the region, his town, Cavaillon, has a market every Monday morning along its main thoroughfare. "It is probably the least charming market of the Luberon," the text reads, "somewhere that locals shop for cut-price clothing, bargain underwear multi-packs, fabrics, leather goods, bedding, bags, household products, etc. As such it is 'real,' but reality probably isn't why you come to the Luberon."

By the time I read this line I felt I knew Sobin well enough to see him smile, shake his head—some gesture to note this irony—the *What-ever* quotation marks around the word "real," the frank sniff that a person doesn't travel to the Luberon looking for reality. Not now perhaps. Though clearly *he* had. Sobin would have relished, I felt certain, that his market town had not succumbed to the creamy charm of artisanal-proud Luberon with its stratospheric land prices for ruined cottages, one of which he had bought decades earlier as a young man looking for poetry.

It wasn't his poetry that let me feel I knew him and could conjure his dry humor. Not even his fiction did that. Though I admired his slim novel, *The Fly-Truffler,* about a widower whose Provençal tradition of hunting truffles allows him to encounter his dead wife in dreamlike meetings while searching in the damp underworld of the woods—there was too much magical realism for me, I suppose, or maybe I was becoming allergic to widow books, determined never to write one. Though—look at me.

It was Sobin's essays that grabbed me. His final work. Appropriately, for someone who had written a novel making a metaphor of finding the reclusive truffle hidden underground, and for a man who watched as the ancient quiet of the region he had chosen for its reclusiveness flipped into a real estate boom, his essays are about what he calls "vestiges," the bare traces of prehistoric and medieval life in his adopted landscape. The world before change overwhelmed the furthest, deepest reach of history.

He often found these vestiges as he walked the isolated territory near his home in the Vaucluse, and in his reading of obscure accounts of the region, memoirs, old civic documents, scientific papers. His essays are about these encounters with the deep past—the lost, invisible past beyond memory and reckoning. He delicately stitches together tatters of the historical fabric rent by time.

Breathtaking essays, reconstructing (it's tempting to say *resurrecting*) Provençal fossils, while never letting go the urgency of inquiry into the buried past we live atop. "Obscure, usually encrusted, more often than not illegible," he says, "these artifacts . . . establish points from which we might situate our own existence today."

Who cares about fossils? Not me. Even Sobin admits laconically that "for myself, the past per se holds little interest, and the present offers only the profound malaise of a culture increasingly devoid of the protocols of self-reflection." Another leisure man, for isn't it leisure alone that safeguards reflection? That cloistered nun years ago, maybe she started all this (*you and your nuns*). I had asked her what her way of life was based upon—love of God, the search for meaning? What was the foundation of contemplative life? *Oh,* she said, without a pause—*leisure, it's based on leisure.* I put her in a book years ago. And here she is again. Bears repeating.

She didn't say her life was *about* leisure, but based on it. Sobin's fossils, his shards and chips, don't expose the recondite obsession of a pedant. They form a lens of penetrating inquiry. His essays bring forward what archaeologists uncover with their tiny brushes, their manicure-set tools and their infinite patience. But he does it in language—a world lost but still *there*. Which is to say, here.

It's important to the power of these prose pieces that So-bin is not an expert, that he's determined to understand, sheerly by pondering the evidence, what is hidden in the charnel house we live upon. That's why they're essays, and not studies. Why they pulse with urgency, and are humble and passionate, even as he is grateful, almost reverent about the scholars and paleontologists he counts on for expertise.

I read all these late books—*Luminous Debris, Ladder of Shadows*—and brought along on the trip the bare sheaf of pages that comprises the final one, *Aura: Last Essays*. He had more essays projected, and in the thin trail of sentences at the end of *Aura,* his widow—his editor—provides an appendix of these unfinished, perhaps even unstarted essays: an account of a trip he planned to undertake following the exact pathways of Petrarch's 1336 ascent of nearby Mont Ventoux; an essay on the scarcity of light in medieval homes and the sacredness invested in candles and oil lamps; an essay on leprosy, another on the "extrasensory function of church bells." On and on his inquisitiveness goes in this list of unwritten essays—pieces about "Madder: The Color That Vanished," about Van Gogh's Arles bedroom, another on "Charles Plumier and the Adamic Naming of Flora" (another person seeing the botanist as organizing angel). Finally, "The Death of Provençal," the last in his billowing list of anticipated essays, "a long essay," his final notation says, "recounting the last liminal traces of a language and, inseparably, a millennial culture on the very point of vanishing altogether."

Vanishing altogether. The very thing he was in the process of doing as he listed these never-to-be-written essays. He had found his subject, and his form—the traces of lived life—vestiges, a stone, a fossilized bone, a statue's torso.

In these prose pieces, he moves beyond his earlier literary forms (poems, novels) to the mind itself—ruminative pieces recounting his fascinated study of loss and remembrance as evidenced in the bones and shards of Provence. What he calls vestiges are the physical evidence of what I've been calling, in narrative terms, vignettes. Both prove the enduring presence of life in the teeth of death, in the lived aftermath of death's reality. The fossil. The bone chip. The memory of the hand grasping mine. They are still here somehow, not quite lost to the touch.

And so Sobin, who came to deep France to be a poet, finally becomes an essayist, heir to Montaigne. He retired early to his cottage, if not to a château—seeking the reflective mind, its presence in life and history, and in himself. Looking not for "a self," that thing modernity keeps saying we're looking for when that is the last thing we need, choking on our individuality. Looking for his mind.

"There is a need . . . to situate ourselves in regard to our own evolving," Sobin writes, trying to explain his dedication to obscure texts and buried bones. The dead are not about death. I get that. Now. But he is making the point not as personal recognition of loss and its uses, but as history, on this stretch of land where the model of the human, lost and lost and lost yet again, layer upon lost layer—is found in the patient pursuit of vestiges over time.

"Reading books, visiting museums, or simply stopping short before the vast, gold umbrella of some chestnut tree in mid-autumn," he says, "aren't we always, in a sense, looking for ourselves?" And who would that be? Not the psychological self, musing over its wounds, mother, father, faithless friends, lovers, the *What-ever* of personal history.

You weren't for any of that either. *Free your mind,* you'd say. *Let go of all that stuff.* We loved Sobin—oh, right, you weren't part of that. I found him on my own. After.

Sobin's essays display a contemporary Montaigne mind pondering, interpreting. The job of being human is not figuring things out, but getting lost in thought. Isn't that what holding a vestige to the light is? Holding a vignette in mind? Shards, bits. Considering them, lost in thought. A wonderful figure of speech, you said one day when the phrase came up, wry and amused as you often were by a turn of phrase (the first gift you gave me: a dictionary, followed soon after by a thesaurus). Isn't thought supposed to *find* something, find an answer? But *lost in thought* is where we often were, where we wanted to be, you and I across the yellow kitchen table, another cup of coffee.

Annette and I motored on to Bordeaux, stood before the giant statues of Montaigne and Montesquieu facing off in the yawning Place des Quinconces like two figures made of salt. Somehow a city—even Montaigne's city (he had been the mayor of Bordeaux)—was not for us. Back to the Route du Foie Gras, into the tourist town of Sarlat, birthplace of Montaigne's beloved friend Étienne de La Boétie whose house, wedged into a turn, facing the main square and rising to a peaked roof, is marked with a historic plaque, the whole area chockablock with shops selling—what else?—jars of foie gras.

Had his beloved friend lived—no essays. Or so Montaigne felt. Death and loss threw him into the imaginary friendship of "meddling with writing." But Étienne de La Boétie did die, in 1563, only thirty-two, leaving behind a handful of writings, on the subject of political intelligence and power, that Montaigne revered. "I know no one who can be compared with him," Montaigne writes in "Of Friendship," an early essay. "If you press me to tell why I loved him," he says, "I feel that this cannot be expressed, except by answering: Because it was he, because it was I."

Love, they say, is a constant interrogation. Montaigne says it differently: "Friendship feeds on communication." But love is not an *answer* to anything. Friendship of the sort Montaigne speaks of (and experienced) is "a harmony of wills," he says. Being together, getting lost—in each other, lost in each other's thoughts.

It was windy in Sarlat, the narrow streets crammed with narrow shops stacked with tins and jars of goose liver pâté, whole alarming lobes of pale livers in their shrink-wrapped jackets, looking as if they might start pulsing outside the plastic. Annette took my picture in front of La Boétie's birthplace, my windbreaker billowing out as if I had been force-fed too, my face seeming to grimace. But that was from the glare of the sun.

In spite of Gustaf Sobin and his vestiges, after we left Sarlat we didn't stop at the museum for the Lascaux caves. But I made a sharp turn off the road when I saw notice of the

Château des Milandes, the grand property of Josephine Baker, who was born in St. Louis in 1905, reborn in the freedom of Paris in the 1920s. She bought the château after the Second World War, filling it with her "rainbow family" of adopted children. We wandered around the giant stony place, hardly any other visitors that day, the gardens and lawns vast, yawning, a whole caged area given over to "birds of prey," falcons and owls, eagles, hawks. The Web site makes it all look like Disneyland, cheery and bright, offering exhibits and events for children. But when we were there, it was a shell of memory, a large forlorn photo of Josephine Baker sitting on the steps by the kitchen the day she was evicted from the place. She was broke, her dream taken from her. Still, her enormous glorioso smile, her lithe body on the postcard I bought. Her radiance. Her bravery. She was awarded the Croix de Guerre for her work with the Resistance, was made a Chevalier of the Légion d'honneur by de Gaulle.

Her indelible image no matter what she lost is evident in the postcard photo—those famous faux bananas strapped around her bare waist like a ring of male trophies stiff with excitement to be encircling her flesh, her lissome form breaking all the rules. You feel the transgressive thrill even now when there seem to be no rules—at least not for nudity onstage.

A visit to the scandalous Josephine Baker, free of St. Louis, shimmying her *danse sauvage* across France—she not only got away from segregation, she achieved the midwestern Elsewhere. This was the right prelude to visiting Montaigne's tower, he who displayed undisguised (*naked*) envy in the *Es-*

sais as he listened to the description of people living naturally, naked and unabashed in "that other world which has been discovered in our century," wishing that he could strip naked in his writing. The only way to write.

Montaigne's château, huge and somehow haughty, is a separate building from the tower. It was completely reconstructed after a fire in 1885 damaged it, the original château built by Montaigne's grandfather. The family was mercantile (fish and wine), only a couple of generations ennobled, his mother apparently from a Spanish converso family.

Any visit to Montaigne's tower is not about the château in any case. He maintained he had no interest in domestic arrangements—unlike his beloved father, Pierre, who spent his life making improvements to the vast place. Montaigne's widow was the last of his family to inhabit it. It remains, as it always has been, a private residence—whose, we didn't know, though as we approached the entrance to the tower, an SUV pulled up, crunching over the sand-colored gravel entry area across the way. Three people, a man and two women, got out and entered the place, as if they had pulled up to an overwrought suburban McMansion, loose-limbed in jeans and windbreakers. They didn't turn toward the tower.

I think we were both startled to see how simple the visiting arrangements for the tower were. At a little outbuilding, almost a hut, a young girl had pointed the way to the tower, down a vaguely tended path with a hand-lettered sign—*Tour*. It seemed that we could just wander in.

Annette said I should have it to myself first, go in alone. *La tour.* There were no other visitors around.

I climbed the staircase, past Montaigne's private chapel that took up the dark entry level, niched with an altar, a shrinelike cavern. And finally, I stood alone in the round room, his library, the light-filled chamber where it all happened, once ringed with books, the stony enclosure where he devised his pieces, some shorter than a page, some long enough to make a chapbook, the writing he called his *Essais*—thinking it was a throwaway word.

The windows never had glass, and he refused to outfit the library with a fireplace (imagine the cold in winter) in order to safeguard his books. The lines of wisdom he had inscribed on the ceiling in Latin and some in Greek had been reinscribed in modern times in a restoration effort. The room was surely emptier (no books) than he knew it. His desk—or a desk—was positioned near the back wall, centered across from the windows on the other wall. A chair pulled neatly up to the desk. Nobody around, no forbidding sign, no ribbon across the chair. I sat in it, feeling slightly criminal nonetheless, or just silly. It was a long way to come to sit in a chair he'd never sat in, regarding an empty room with words on the ceiling I couldn't decipher.

I wandered over to an opening at the side of the room and checked out the adjacent alcove where he had allowed a little fireplace, a cramped space to warm himself. This was the room, a sign said, where he slept. To the side, a kind of chute, a peephole down to the chapel so he could hear—even see—Mass without going down there. So the tower wasn't a "study."

It was almost a bachelor den. What do they call them now?—
a man cave. Except his was a tower, rising, not sinking into
the ground.

The chapel—the fact of it—surprised me. That the habits
of religion—the old cult of Catholicism, not the new freedom
of Protestant individual faith—mattered to him so much. He
built liturgy into his privacy, this first "modern man," this
man we claim as a skeptic. He was a skeptic—and also a believer. He bridged the gap. He lived above with his books in
the unheated tower, and he tended, faithfully, the rituals
down there in the candlelit dark where mystery abided.

On the walls of the alcove bedroom I made out what was
left of the painted frescoes (naked nymphs and godlets
mostly, bundles of chipped floral décor) and the graffiti of
earlier visitors—boldly scrawled *Emma 1882* and *Pierre 1920,*
and someone whose name and message I couldn't decipher,
the date 1989, the most recent I found.

I looked out the window of the alcove to experience (or
think I was experiencing) his view. A great blossoming *mar-
ronnier,* part of an allée of lofting chestnuts marshaled along
a gravel path leading to the tower where I was, where he had
been—with or possibly without chestnuts, or these chestnuts
anyway. Nearer by, just below, a triangular untended parterre
garden where it was easy to imagine herbs in careful arrays.
That parterre garden sent a brief thrill through me—*that,* I
thought, could have been here when he was here, could have
been what he looked down upon. Because surely he ate
well—he tells us he loved rich sauces, delicately flavored.

I turned back toward the main room, his writing room. I

wanted to take some descriptive notes, hoping for an insight for the book I was—I am—writing (an earnest essayist acting the part—*notes . . . the ineluctable consequence of one's greatest inward energy*). The parterre of herbs was a start, but what else? Turning quickly, gaze angled down to the notebook where I was drawing the shape of the triangular garden, I misjudged the doorway (an earlier century, a smaller scale) and smacked my head—hard—into the stone wall, just above *Pierre 1920.*

You do see stars. Or bits of white, spinning, that you could take for stars.

Then, in my bell-ringing, star-shooting brain, I remembered—how had I forgotten?—that Montaigne had whacked his head too, colliding with another rider, momentarily knocked unconscious, slammed off his horse as he rode this wooded property. He was taken for dead as his men carried him, insensible, back to the château. It is one of the few recognizably memoiristic vignettes in the *Essais,* a scrupulous reconstruction of a pivotal episode, a bit of story in the midst of all his pages of musing, pondering, reflecting, wondering—what used to be called philosophizing.

He started his project in this room in imitation of the ancients, his beloved (and much memorized) classical writers, especially the Stoics. His belief—the title of an early essay—was nothing less than that "To Philosophize Is to Learn to Die," life's essential lesson. The early essays, after his "retirement" to the tower, after Étienne de La Boétie's death, after his own little death when he was knocked off his horse, the death from which he returned—all these early essays are about how to die. Dying with honor. Remember that? The airless airplane, the delivery room nurse stroking my hand, you holding the other: *You aren't dying, you're having a panic attack.* That's how Montaigne started—with death and its approach.

Why did he honor this crashing moment, so uncharacteristically, with narrative? Well, it was a near-death experience. But even more, it was that most literary of experiences—unbiddable, decisive—the turn that allowed him to pierce to the core of the imagination, perhaps for the first time. In being knocked off his horse, he experienced the doubleness necessary to empower personally voiced writing. He experienced the fall—but he also *observed* the fall. Both. In separate but related strands of consciousness he experienced and he saw the experience.

The shock of this double register galvanized him to note the parallels of experience and observation. It was a kind of conversion moment. (No wonder that most notorious conversion—Saint Paul's—is represented as a fall from his horse. Neither the fall nor the horse is mentioned in the Bible, but this is the standard image of his change of heart, as if the violence of being knocked down from a height were the only way to express it adequately. In a sense, Paul's fall inaugurates the Christian era, a tumble from a smooth power ride, a thump out of the tribal self into a vision of a united world.)

You get knocked off balance, off your assumptions. You see stars. Or what you take for stars—because anything this overwhelming catapults you into poetry, into metaphor. Your life changes, is changed. Even in our homely cliché we speak of being *struck* by this or that. The point is you *see*—a fresh kind of seeing that feels accurate because the self is not, for once, a subject, not a weight you're lugging around, a slave to experience it must either endure or enjoy. This self is revealed as an instrument that can render, if not "reality," then the experience of reality. The poetry of experience fastens to the reportage of the world.

To express experience accurately you must, paradoxically, be knocked out of yourself—knocked out of the inevitable narcissism and egotism that is our narrative lot. The small-ness of the self. This quicksilver experience has been given, by literature and psychology, the lackluster label *detachment*. Or as Keats called it, also fastening on an unwieldy phrase, *Negative Capability*. By which he meant in a letter to his brother that one must be "capable of being in uncertainties, Mysteries, doubts, without any irritable reaching after fact and reason." And how is that done? By acquiescing to the leisure that apparently is so elusive, but is the key to "the life of the mind." It is impossible to corral this experience in a name, a term, but once felt, there is nothing—not even love—to compare.

Montaigne's younger brother had been hit on the head too—that tennis ball to the temple. He didn't experience (so far as we know) detachment. He died of the blow. So perhaps Montaigne had an astonished, even slightly grateful/guilty sense of dumb luck in surviving his fall because, unlike his brother, he "came to." But surely he registered as well—his description of the experience proves this—the significance of his head wound: it gave him a new, enlarged consciousness.

In his *Essais* he found the purpose of this self: to see and then to say.

The personal essay was born of a smack upside the head.

It is a cruel irony (is there any other kind?) that Montaigne's purposely evasive word for his writings—*essais*—has become the dread-dreary term associated with freshman English, the term paper, the school "theme." Is cigarette smoking harmful to your health? Discuss. Welcome back to school, children—describe your summer vacation. And until quite recently try to tell an editor who has professed to admire your novel that you have "a book of essays" in the drawer. It was long the genre that dared not speak its name in the literary marketplace.

Not Montaigne's fault. His book was an immediate best seller. He thought he had liberated writing (or at least himself) from literary formality, to be wild, untamed, eccentric, the last thing we think of now when we hear the word "essay," that domesticated homework pet. He could just as easily have called his pieces his *What-evers*. His use of the word *essais* was meant to be just that offhand and undefined. What he had in mind in his attempt (that word again—attempt, try, *essai*) was to renew the springs of the first-person voice bounding across the field of what we keep calling, against our uncertainty, reality. But "reality" and individual experience are exactly what smack together (in the head, then on the page) in the essay. The personal and the public find perfect register—for the length of the thing, the length of the try.

Americans in particular love the first-person voice. It's no coincidence that our greatest poem is "Song of Myself." We also seem to favor first-person narrators for our classic novels—*Call me Ishmael . . . You don't know about me without you have read a book by the name of* The Adventures of Tom Sawyer; *but that ain't no matter . . .* And Fitzgerald, of course—*After Gatsby's death the East was haunted for me like that, distorted beyond my eyes' power of correction. So when the blue smoke of brittle leaves was in the air and the wind blew the wet laundry stiff on the line I decided to come back home . . .*

Or maybe we don't "love" the personal voice—we just can't help trusting it. It feels authentic to us, a people given the charge in our founding document to pursue happiness, that individual enterprise. It may be our greatest fiction—to believe the personal voice is more "authentic" than other narrative modes. We'll take it, most of the time, over "omniscience." Not only because we are a notoriously self-regarding people, but because the first-person voice opens the narrative door to speculation and reflection. Not to knowing, but to wondering. Perhaps we don't just want a story. We want to know how it feels, how it seems. We want the story of thinking. How much of *Moby Dick* is "story," and how much a vast tract, an ocean of essay, waves and swells of speculation attached to the adventure tale of the great white whale?

This is my letter to the world that never wrote to me—another poetic parent of the personal voice, speaking in her sidelong way (*Tell the truth, but tell it slant*).

Famously, rather coquettishly, Dickinson also said, *I'm nobody—who are you?* That apparent self-revelation (really a self-screening) and its waggish question display the economy shared by the personal voice in lyric poetry and the personal essay (two forms up to the same business). Of course you're nobody (so am I). But that fragile voice reveals more than a self. It holds the mirror up—not to itself but to the world.

The essay is a solo dance, a private pirouette, its glowing footstep emerging onto the public street, as we saw it that rainy night across from the Sorbonne, you holding the black umbrella over me as I snapped the iPhone, while you took shallow breaths, telling me to take all the time I needed.

To Stay

If I neglect to take my flashlight up to the monastery chapel for Vespers, I will regret it later when, sloshing blindly through puddles left in the rutted dirt road by the recent downpours, I stumble back in the dark to my—hermitage. Hard not to stumble over the word rising like a medieval hiccup in the middle of my smoothly ticking postmodern life.

A note I've just found in an old journal from a weeklong retreat I took several years ago.

Unlike Montaigne's tower, there's no private chapel in my study at home. Home. The weeklong retreat interrupted my own life "down there," as I thought of home. Or thought of you—you were still here. Or there, waving from the porch as I streaked off, the dog by your side.

I was on a mountain in California, thinking my thoughts— or rather, trying not to think them for once. I was living not simply "away," in a geographic sense, but out of time, out of modernity, in a monastery over the great western coast.

Though I'd come halfway across the country from Minnesota, I wasn't really traveling. I'd come here to stay put.

Meanwhile, the world revved along down there, and inside me too—so many choices all jumbled together. We have chosen a problematical name for ourselves: we are no longer souls as we once were, not even citizens; we're all consumers now, grasping all the *stuff* every which way. *Only connect,* E. M. Forster (who was a modernist) instructed. A few generations of only connecting, and here we are, grabbing and stuffing. Order isn't our thing. We aren't the Ladies, adhering to a careful System. We aren't Mendel, cycling through the Holy Hours, tending generations of edible peas, season to season. We definitely aren't Montaigne, retreating to his château. But still, that was the idea of the week. Retreat.

What a strange fin de siècle we were passing through when I went there, fearful, terrorized, badly shaken the second year of the new millennium. Montaigne retreated to his tower in his perilous times. But for us the word *tower* has an ominous meaning. *The Towers came down.*

Strangely, after all this time of being a country—a "great" country—Americans still prefer the idea of a future to the idea of history. We resist the limitations of history, its overwhelming weight, the denial of self-determination. We're in charge, aren't we? "The only superpower left," we said for that brief *entre deux guerres* period from the fall of the Berlin Wall to the fall of the Twin Towers. The vanity of imperial glitter rubs off on us, a gold dust the world longs for and resents. We've even elected a leader with a fixation on gold and gilt. We can't help preening: we've created ourselves. We're nobody's memory.

In a way, the idea of the future *is* our history. The filmy future is a can-do place, our natural habitat. Whereas the past is distressingly complete, full of our absence. We seem to know that if you take history too seriously, you'll never escape it. In place of national memory we have substituted the only other possible story form, the dream. And the essential thing required of the American dream has always been that it must remain a dream, vivid, tantalizingly beyond reach. Just the dreaming of it—which costs nothing, absolutely nothing except every cent of our imaginative attention—inflates the soul. Fills it, rather than fulfills it.

We wish to be free—whatever that means—and we know that memory, personal or civic, does not promote freedom. Gustaf Sobin felt he had to leave America to hold a bit of Neolithic bone, to find human memory—that is, history. Memory tethers.

I was living—a week, almost two, tourist time again—in a niche of memory. Cultural, not personal, memory. It was Lent, and I had come to California on retreat. Was given a hermitage, a small trailer. Prefab, wood paneled, tidy. A cell, as the monks call their own hexagonal hermitages that surround the chapel farther up the steep hill. The idea is not prison cell, but honeybee cell. A hive busy with the *opus Dei,* the life of prayer.

For those days I was following a way of life, balanced on a pattern of worship trailing back to Saint Benedict and his sixth-century Rule for monasteries. And still further back, into the Syrian desert where the solitary weirdos starved and prayed themselves out of history their own mystic way. Benedict's Rule drew all that eccentric urgency into the social embrace. Into civic life, and finally into history. He took the savage hermitage of the Levant and trained it into the European monastery. Made a center out of the raw margin of the early desert recluses. The convent, after all, says frankly what it is: a convention, part of the social compact that claims order as a minion of tradition.

The monastic day in California in the early twenty-first century, like the monastic day at Monte Cassino early in the sixth century, is poised on a formal cycle of prayers that revolves with the seasons, the same Office of Hours Gregor Mendel shaped his life around. A system still rolling along. It divides (or connects) the day (and night) by a series of communal prayer liturgies. This day, like all days, is a memory of the day that preceded. The day is a habit, the hours reinscribed as ritual. The days softly folded into seasons, each with meaning, feast and fast, sorrow, jubilation.

Memory, habit, ritual: those qualities that do not perhaps sustain "life" (which is elemental, fiercely chaotic), but *a way of life,* bound to time with the silken ties of—what else?— words. The West murmurs, trying to locate itself; the East breathes, trying to lose itself. (The Buddhists are down the coast highway at Tassajara, meditating silently, eating intelligently.)

A simplistic distinction, not entirely accurate. After all, the heart of Western contemplative life is silence, and the East, in at least one central practice, chews the word, the mantra. Still, Christianity is undeniably a wordy religion.

Lectio divina, sacred reading, the ancient practice laid down by the early patristic writers, is alive still today; it is part of the daily routine here.

Augustine, whose *Confessions* I've brought along, is the most passionate exemplar of this practice, not simply one of the West's great writers, but its greatest reader. The year is 397, and he is composing the West's first autobiography in North Africa, creating the genre that lies at the core of Western consciousness, substituting in place of the ancient idea of the *story,* the modern literary idea of *a life.* The omniscient authority of the tale told around the campfire turns to ash in the burning cry of the first-person voice.

Augustine is, like every memoirist who follows him, hot with his subject. He's inflamed with the account of his fascinatingly bad life turned mysteriously good. But he only gives this story the first nine of the thirteen books of his *Confession.* Then, without explanation or apology, as if it were the most natural thing in the world, the work glides smoothly into an extended meditation—call it a long essay—on the book of Genesis, as if this too were "his life."

In fact, the movement from his life to his reading isn't smooth—it's ablaze too. The narrative becomes more, not less, urgent. *His* story, for Augustine, is only part of the story. There is a clear logic dictating the form of the *Confessions* that unites the account of his life with his reading of Genesis, though this is not a logic we moderns see as readily as his late-fourth-century readers would have.

Having constructed himself in the first nine books of the *Confessions,* Augustine rushes on to investigate how God created the universe—how God, that is, created him. And all of us, all of *this*. Reading, therefore, is concentrated life, not a pastiche of life or an alternative to life. The soul, pondering, *is* experience. Augustine, great-grandfather of Montaigne, his autobiography striving toward the essay, poses his questions, wonders—meddles with writing.

Lectio is not "reading" as we might think of it. It is for Augustine, as it was for Ambrose his teacher, and for these California monks in their twenty-first-century cells, an acute form of *listening*. The method is reading—words on paper. But the endeavor is undertaken as a relationship, one filled with the pathos of the West: the individual, alone in a room, puts finger to page, following the Word, and attempts to touch the elusive Lord last seen scurrying down the rabbit hole of creation. *In the beginning God created . . .*

Augustine, grappling with Genesis in his study, is more heated than Augustine struggling famously with "the flesh." He invents autobiography not to reveal his memory of his life, but to plumb the memory of God's creative act.

"My mind burns to solve this complicated enigma," he says with an essayist's anguish more intense than anything in his revelations about his own history. He understands his life as a model of the very creation that is beyond him—and in him. He writes and writes, reads and reads his way through this double conundrum, the mystery of his own biography and the mystery of creation.

He makes the central, paradoxical discovery of autobiography: memory is not in the service of nostalgia. It is the future that commands its presence. It is not a reminiscence, but a quest.

How bizarrely truncated the modern notion of "seeking a self" would seem to Augustine. Autobiography, for him, does not seek a self, not even for its own "salvation." For him, the memory work of autobiography uses the self as the right instrument to seek meaning. That is, to seek God, a.k.a. Ultimate Mystery, the One who, when asked to give his name, says, *I Am That I Am*.

Augustine takes this a step further. On the first page of the *Confessions* he poses a problem that has a familiar modern ring: "It would seem clear that no one can call upon Thee without knowing Thee." There is, in other words, the problem of God's notorious absence. Augustine takes the next step west; he seeks his faith *with* his doubt: "May it be that a man must implore Thee before he can know Thee?" The assumption here is that faith is not to be confused with certainty; the only thing people can really count on is longing and the occult directives of desire. So, Augustine wonders, does that mean prayer must come *before* faith? Illogical as it is, perhaps not-knowing is the first condition of prayer, rather than its negation. Can that be? He finds his working answer in scripture: "How shall they call on Him in Whom they have not believed? . . . they shall praise the Lord that seek Him."

Praise, he decides, antedates certainty—as well as faith. Longing, not "belief," is the core of self that unfurls its song, the instinct to cry out. Poetry.

This is where the Psalms come in. They are praise. More: they are relation, full of the intensity of intimacy, rage, petulance, and joy, the sheer delight and exasperation of close encounter. This is the spectrum of all emotion, all life. The Psalmist reaches with his lyric claw to fetch it all in words.

Words, words, words. They circle and spin around West-ern spiritual practice. They abide. They even sustain a way of life—this monastic one—careening down the centuries, cre-ating families (the Benedictines, the Franciscans, the Car-melites, and others) with unbroken lineages longer than any royal house in Europe. The pattern of prayer, handed down generation to generation, has sustained this extraordinary lifeline. Words have proven to be more protean than blood.

The monastic life of the West cleaves to the Psalms, claiming the ancient Jewish poetry as its real heart, more central to its day than the New Testament or the sacraments. The Psalms keep this life going—the verbal engine running into the deepest recess of Christian social life, and beyond that back into the source of silence, the desert of the early hermits. The idea here in this American monastery, based on a tenth-century reformation of the earlier Benedictine model, is to wed both traditions—the social monastery and the soli-tary hermitage, city and desert, public and private. It is a way of life based on a historical pattern.

Therefore, this life might be understood as a living mem-ory. It is also a life lived, literally, within poetry. And as it happens, the name of this prefab hermitage where I have been lodged is Logos. The Word. The word made home. A week in the word.

Against one wall, the single bed. I make it quickly like a good novice first thing every morning, pulling the dorm-room spread square. Suitcase stowed beneath—I'm here long enough to want to obscure the truth: I'm a visitor, passing through. I've never liked being a traveler: I take up residence. *Found us a château yet?* you'd say as I scrolled through real estate listings for the south of France. "I'm going home," I say instinctively, returning to my hotel the first day in a foreign city. So, here: Logos is home.

Also a round table (eat, read, write, prop elbows on). Shelves niched in next to the tiny open closet space where I've installed my books, what I could lug on the plane: Montaigne of course. Also a new novel by someone that someone else said was good (not opened); poems I have long loved—James Wright, W. S. Merwin; Augustine with his bookmark; Dawson's *Religion and the Rise of Western Culture*; a dictionary that didn't have the only word I've looked up so far. And Thich Nhat Hanh with yet another volume attempting to calm us westerners down, out of ourselves: breathe, feel, exhale—there. And like everybody on a desert island, the Bible (the New Jerusalem version), whether I'll read it or not.

A rudimentary kitchen runs along another wall, tiny bathroom beyond that, the only other room. And two windows, one to nowhere, hugged by two crowded eucalyptus trees and the vinca-covered curve of the steep eroded dirt road I climb to the chapel. The other window, the window that counts, gives onto . . . paradise. The western rind of America peels off far below into the extravagant white curl of Big Sur. The slant of the Santa Lucia range, where we are perched, cuts off the view of the coast highway, but the Pacific, blue as steel (it is overcast) or ultramarine (on sunny days), appears to be cantilevered below us, a blue platform leading to the end of the world. Sometimes, roughed up by wind and whitecaps, the ocean loses this quality of being architecture; it becomes expensive fabric, shimmering, silvered. Then, simply, what it is: the vast pool, brimming to the horizon.

This is where I came. There was no crisis. No, at the moment, heartache or career impasse. You were still there, still in place, "holding the fort," you said, waving me off on yet another trip. No dark night except the usual ones. Doesn't everyone wake up maybe two nights a week, mind gunning, palms sweating? In the eyes-open misery of night, sensation gets mashed to a paste of meaninglessness—life's or one's own. No anguish beyond that to report. Every so often I just do this: go on retreat.

This is not uncommon in our supposedly secular age. Meditation, massage, monasteries, spas—the postmodern stomach, if not its soul, knows it needs purging. Such places are popular, booked months in advance. Down the coast the Buddhists were meditating, stemming herbs thoughtfully. Esalen was nearby too, and the place where Henry Miller discovered the hot tub. I could have gone to the Buddhists, cleansed in the silence, approached the big Empty that is the great source. That, after all, is my God.

But I came here, to follow the Christian monastic day laid out like a garden plot by Benedict at the close of the Roman era. I'm Western, I like my silence sung.

The days were silent. The only words were the chanted ones in the chapel, unless I called home. My thin voice sounded odd, insubstantial. When I called, you recited all the messages from my office answering machine. I asked if you were okay. You were. You? Me too, I'm okay. I love you. Me too—I love *you*. Touching base. The telephone receiver clicked back into its cradle, and the mirage of news and endearments melted. It didn't disappear exactly—I left the telephone room, a little booth by the monastery bookstore, smiling, your voice in my ear.

It's just that conversation, in that place (that vacuum) became a bare tissue of meaning, a funny human foible. The midday bell was ringing, and there was something I was trying to remember.

That's wrong. I wasn't trying "to remember" something. More like this: I was being remembered. Being remembered into a memory—beyond history to the inchoate, still intense trace of feeling that first laid down this pattern.

The memory that puts all personal memory in the shade. Praying or chanting the Psalms draws me out of whatever I might be thinking or remembering (for so much thinking *is* remembering, revisiting, rehearsing).

The first morning bell rings at 5:30. I walked up to the chapel in the dead-of-night dark for Vigils, the first round of daily prayers. The chapel is stark, perhaps to some eyes severe. To me, though, the calm of invitation. I bow, as each of the monks does when he enters, toward the dark sanctuary where a candle burns. The honey-colored wood chairs and benches, ranked on two sides, face each other. They form two barely curved lines, two choirs deftly passing the ball of chant back and forth across the arched room as, somewhere beyond us, the sun rises and the world begins to exist again.

How it was those days: my mind wanders. There are the monks, uniformed into similarity by their cream-colored robes, and yet I manage to wonder about them. Is that one in the back gay? The one with the clipped accent next to me— maybe from Boston? The one on his left looks like a banker, could have been a CEO, why not? The guy across looks like a truck driver. On and on it goes, my skittery mind. Meanwhile, the Psalms keep rolling. A line snags—*More than the watchman for daybreak, my whole being hopes in the Lord*— and I am pulled along.

It's also boring. What happens in the chapel partakes of tedium. It must. The patterns repeat and return. Every four weeks the entire book of Psalms, all 150 poems, is chanted. And then begun again, and again, and again. *Sing to the Lord a new song,* we have been saying since David was king. This new song rolls from the rise of monotheism, unbroken, across the first millennium, through the second, now the third, the lapidary waves of chant polishing the shore of history. There are men here—there are men and women in monasteries all over the world—repeating this pattern in antiphonal choirs, softly lobbing this same language back and forth to each other. What *is* this invisible globe they are passing across the space?

Worship. But what is worship? It is the practice of the fiercest possible attention. And here, new millennium, the ancient globe of polished words, rubbed by a million voices down the centuries, is the filmy glass of memory. Memory understood not as individual story, not as private fragment clutched to the heart, trusted only to the secret page. Even in the midst of high emotion, the rants and effusions that characterize the Psalmist's wild compass, there is a curious non-psychological quality to the voice. This is the voice of inner experience. It has no mother, no father. Or it borrows the human family as its one true relation. These words express the memory of the world's longing. Desire so elemental that its shape can only be glimpsed in the incorruptible storehouse of poetic image—*he sends ice crystals like bread crumbs, and who can withstand that cold? Our days pass by like grass, our prime like a flower in bloom. A wind comes, the flower goes . . .*

Paging through a picture book of Christian and Buddhist monasteries in the bookstore, stopped by this cutline accompanying a photograph of a beautiful Buddhist monastery, a remark by a *dogen:* "The only truth is we are here now." The physical beauty of the Buddhist place is eloquent, revealing the formal attentiveness of a supreme aesthetic: mindfulness. The human at its best. The food is famous there.

They are living their profound injunction, honoring the fleet moment, and the smallest life: Buddhist retreatants are asked not to kill the black flies that torment them. Here, when I told the monk at the bookstore that ants were streaming all over the kitchen counter of Logos, he handed me an aerosol canister of Raid, and I was glad. I sprayed, mopped, discarded the little poppyseed carcasses. Sat back satisfied, turning again to Montaigne and the mind of the West, figuring, figuring. The sweetish spume of bug spray hung in the air for a day.

The bug spray has to stop, we know that. Contemplative nuns have told me that without the introduction of Buddhist meditation practice into their own lives, they wouldn't be in the monastery anymore. "It's thanks to Buddhism that I'm a Catholic," one of them said. I have never visited an American Christian monastery that did not have Buddhist meditation mats and pillows somewhere in the chapel. The light touch of the missionary work of the East, the absence of cultural imperialism, the poetry of its gestures: the bell is never "struck," never "hit." In the Buddhist monastery, it is invited to sound.

But still this handing down of words, this Western practice I would not wish myself out of. *The only truth is we are here now.* I don't believe we are only here *now.* How could I, transfixed by memory as I am, believing in the surge of these particular words down the channel of the centuries?

Montaigne in his cold tower: *I don't portray being, I portray passing.* Or the Psalmist's way of saying that: *I will ponder the story of your wonders.*

We enter the dark sanctuary, bow to the flame, assemble in the honey-colored chairs again, two halves of the human choir. Some mornings at Vigils, before first light, it feels strangely as if our little band—fifteen monks, a handful of retreatants—are legion. The two facing choir lines curve slightly, two horizon lines, the bare sketch of a sphere, the world coming into being.

We greet first light, we enter dark night. It is all very old, a memory of a memory. And it is new as only the day can be new, over and over. The day is a paradox, and we enter it possessed by time's tricky spirit, history and the present instant sublimely transposed.

We are here now, the East is chanting from its side of the monastery.

And so for now, the West chants in response, the antiphon rising as it has all these centuries, out of the ancient memory we inhabit together, *Sing a new song, sing a new song. . . .*

A lone in a room with words—that's how I've thought of Montaigne in his tower. How I've always thought of writing—anyone writing. Solitude is not only "at the heart" of writing. It *is* the heart. These days, months, staring at the screen, notebooks with their crabbed lines—this *meddling with writing.* A person needs to be alone to do this thing— even if Grace Paley infuriatingly said that she wrote just fine on the train, going home to the Village after teaching a full load at Sarah Lawrence in Bronxville.

But then there may be no more solitary location in America than a New York subway—take a look at the faces of those commuters, their heads bent to their open books like monks at their breviaries, little glowing screens casting an otherworldly aura onto their intent faces. They are elsewhere. They are alone. Alone with words as much as any writer at a notebook or screen.

A writer even needs to *pine* for solitude, court it, steal it away from the rest of so-called real life. It's very lover-like, this romance with solitude. It may be the prerequisite that sustains a writing life, more important than talent or discipline, this passion for solitude, the ground upon which the life of the mind roots and blossoms. Solitude is the beguiling illicit love luring us away from the proper marriage of domestic demands and delights or the civic responsibilities of citizenship.

In a moment of great tenderness I once confessed—I wonder if you remembered this—that I loved living with you. *It's like being alone,* I said happily. You cocked your beautiful brow and said mildly, *I gather that's a compliment?*

Being alone with another—it's the greatest love transaction. Being alone is, we know, the best chance you have to be yourself, which is in turn the seed of integrity and of any possible originality.

I fell hard and early for Rilke's line from his 1904 *Letters to a Young Poet,* the standard poetic operating manual for me in my twenties. Rilke describes the ideal relationship as *a love that consists in this, that two solitudes protect and touch and greet each other.* Not until much later did I cock my own brow at this soulful maxim from a man who abandoned his wife and child and spent years mooching around the castles and palaces of admiring countesses and grand dames of the Hapsburg Empire only too happy to give him a room with a view and three squares a day as he contemplated his writing block, alone in his well-appointed room, taking in the magnificent view of the Adriatic.

But never mind that feminist smirk—it came later. Besides poetry, I was studying typography and the handmade book as a grad student. I chose Rilke's line about those two loving solitudes as the first sentence I set, letter by metal letter, from the California job case, the big divided box filled with its "sorts," as typographers call the tiny sculptural letters used to make up words. Composing stick in one hand, picking up tiny bits of molten lead with the other, I was learning to do pretty much what Gutenberg did when he set the first movable type.

This method was how words made their way to press and paper for centuries until very recently when the scribing of digital bits descended upon us and changed the speed of everything in our you've-got-mail culture. The earlier composing method was slow and created an aura of isolation. Just the words and me, one metal letter at a time, laid in the flat of my hand, line by meticulous line, as if even prose were poetry, lineated. You had to consider the spaces as well, as if silence were an essential aspect of language, which of course it is.

I may have taken up my fascination with typography after I read that part of Virginia Woolf's mental health regime— devised by the uxorious Leonard Woolf after one of her ruinous breakdowns—was to learn to set type. Talk about two solitudes protecting each other. Or at least one protecting the other. Leonard was right—setting type by hand is calming. It's sanity-promoting detail work.

This therapeutic hobby led to the founding of the Hogarth Press. Its first volume, printed in 1917 on a little hand press set up on the Woolf dining room table, was composed of a story by Virginia and one by Leonard. The second book, which I long to own or at least hold in my hand, was published in an edition of three hundred in 1918, the beautiful New Zealand short story "Prelude" by Katherine Mansfield, whose work, Virginia admitted in her diary, was the only writing she had ever envied. This typesetting, a solo, silent endeavor (rather like the obsessive knitting that was also a passion among that crowd of modernist writers that included D. H. Lawrence, a demon knitter), turned into the Hogarth Press, a major literary presence in the first half of the twentieth century, and still a literary imprint.

It started with a woman in danger of losing her mind, sequestered in the quiet of a suburban London house, holding a composing stick, as if palming sanity, silently stacking up metal letters to make a line of sense. This is where we get that psycholiterary term—when we speak of someone being "out of sorts." It's a typesetting term: being out of sorts, for a typesetter, means not having enough letters—"sorts" in your job case, perhaps having used up all the p's or q's—so you cannot compose the word you need. Watching your p's and q's—another typesetting metaphor, the two metal bits easy to mistake in the job case. Virginia Woolf was sorting herself out. It worked for a while, quite a while, really. She was alone not only with words, but with their steely components, individual letters. Literary sanity was there, she held it in her thin hand.

I vant to be alone, my mother used to say distractedly, invoking Greta Garbo, when we were making too much havoc at home. In fact, Garbo had not said she wanted to be alone. She said, *I want to be let alone*. But in our own speedy culture, the distinction between the two statements, even for someone not savaged by celebrity, has been conflated. Hurry, hurry, we have all turned into the White Rabbit, and we're very late for a very important date—though most of the time we can't say what it is. For us, *I vant to be alone* means I want to be off the grid, no iPhone, no email, the 24/7 connectivity of our lot. I want to be let alone to *be* alone. No wonder that, to a writer—to readers, to so many beset people now—solitude suggests not loneliness, but serenity, that kissing cousin of sanity. We speak of being alone to recharge our batteries—even in our reach for solitude we seem unable to unplug from the metaphor of our connectivity.

Yet here's the greater paradox: writing, though performed alone, starting in the dark of the mind, is also the only absolutely declarative, meaning-beset art form we have, and its purpose is to communicate. With others. More than a painter, much more than a composer, a writer can never be alone. Our very medium is held in common, the language we are born into (or adopt—Conrad, Nabokov, Aleksandar Hemon from their Slavic languages into English; Milan Kundera from Czech to French; most recently Jhumpa Lahiri from English to Italian).

Language is a shared resource, not individual, not unique, not self-made. We are crowded on all sides with words we hold in common, words that mean the same thing to all of us. We get huffy about grammar, we fight over usage. Language is not, like paint, a medium. It is a system. Another system—

the Ladies with theirs, Gregor Mendel quietly seeking the inner system of generation, the monks spinning the wheel of the cycle of Psalms. Language is the ultimate system. We all use those same twenty-six letters. This is why Gutenberg's invention of movable type works at all.

It is also why people will blithely say to a writer who has spent six or eight years sweating out a work of fiction, "You know, if I had the time, I'd write a novel too." Not something a music lover is likely to tell a composer—"If I had the time, I'd write a symphony." We know we all *own* this thing, this habit of naming, expressing, connecting the narrative dots. The jabber that is our human signifier. I can talk, therefore I can write. If I had the time. If I bothered. In spite of everything I know about how hard it is to write, I can't say I really have an argument against that presumption. You could write this book—if you had the time. If you even cared to. I find it hard to disbelieve this.

But the paradox of a writer's relation to being alone, and specifically being alone with words, is even deeper than the fact that writing is communication. A writer is aware not only of her own voice humming along, but hears with the ear of that mysterious other, the elusive reader for whom the sentences are laid out. Writers are always—always—in relationship. We write to—for—the reader. Which is more confounding, really, than having, as actors do, an *audience* that is a distanced and objectified congregated other.

Writers are caught—how else to put this?—in an embrace. They—we, I—cannot escape from communicating. Even so-called (and self-defined) experimental writers who appear not to care about the reader or even disdain him, underscore, even more powerfully in their refusal to play nicely with others, the frustrations of the chaotic self in its struggle with that most shared and social of materials—language. "Yes," Samuel Beckett, Mr. Minimal, said of his work, "in my life, since we must call it so, there were three things, the inability to speak, the inability to be silent, and solitude, that's what I've had to make the best of."

My life—since we must call it so. Beckett would really rather not have his three attributes gathered into anything as repellently autobiographical as "my life." Yet there it is—a writer is composed, perhaps of equal parts, of silence, articulation, and isolation. That's the job. That's the life.

We do not, in the act of composition, have an audience. We have a reader. The writer is the mouth, the reader the ear. The body is language and it is shared. We write to a singular other whom we must allure, embrace, enchant. We are whispering into that singular shell-shaped ear. This is probably inevitable, for our first literary experience is not as a writer, but as a reader. We read as individuals, and as writers we write not for readers in a collective sense, but for what earlier generations frankly called the "dear reader." It's a crazy love affair, this murmuring into the ear of the elusive yet intimate mystery person. Being so intimate, of course it has to be done in private, in the solitude of the lonely mind.

True, there is a performance aspect to it all. We give readings, separating the private act of composition from the act of sharing the work—but that is after the act of composition is over and done, rather like trotting out your precocious five-year-old to the audience, never thinking to present the act of conception to the crowd. When you give a reading in a large full hall, a genuine theater, the audience is entirely in the dark, you the solo spotlighted figure. You can't see them, and they're very quiet out there. You might even jump to hear that weird beast let out its communal ha-ha at something funny you've read to them, to *it*. You are so alone up there, you forget they have been gathered into an audience. Nothing could be further from the dear reader you were writing to in your room.

In the act of writing, the writer is never really alone, even though being alone is the one thing we recognize as our chance for authenticity, for surprising ourselves out of predictability. For thinking. Even writing a diary, Virginia Woolf cannily noted, is not the act of solitude it might seem—we all like to look good to ourselves, even in that privacy. We are our own dear reader.

Solitude provides the illusion—or is it the reality?—of a self. If I'm alone I can think dark thoughts, be real, be phony, try this, try that. Erase, contradict, forge ahead, double back. We all contain multitudes, not just Whitman, not just Montaigne, that master of contradiction.

The longing for solitude is a deeply romantic passion. But then writing is a romantic thing to do, predicated on desire, urgency, and an ideal of human connection, hardly available in what we wistfully call real life. Maybe especially when we are not living alone, when circumstances deny privacy, not to mention solitude, when we are very much in the midst of the demands of family or job—whatever it is that outlaws solitude—perhaps it is especially *then* we are most in love with what solitude seems to provide, what it promises. It promises freedom.

To be alone is to be free—who said that? It's an idea floating around, said by many. But I'm thinking of Julian Barnes, in *Levels of Life,* his memoir of his wife's untimely death from a brain tumor. He quotes a widowed friend who admits that even in her terrible grief she also realizes she is free. Free of what? Free for what?

In his book Barnes performs what might be called a tour of bereavement—that is, enforced solitude. He does not feel free, as his widowed friend admits to feeling. Wisely, he does not see her admission as the absence of grief, but as an aspect of her particular grief. Grief is the unbearable inverse of resonant solitude; it is solitary confinement, now recognized by the human rights commission as torture. Barnes says he cannot be in crowds—they remind him of his isolation. Or Mary Shelley's response to her husband's death: *Solitude was my only consolation—deep, dark, deathlike solitude.* Or as a recently widowed neighbor of mine said, sheepishly, *I just want to stay in my hidey-hole.*

To be denied the beloved, it turns out, is to be denied oneself. *I love living with you. It's like being alone.* That is the radiant paradox of aloneness/connection that a writer (forget "a writer"—a person) must find within, whether beset with children, with the care of elderly withering parents, stuck with a hopeless spouse, with a soul-sapping job, or just burdened with a killer to-do list. We must learn to be alone in the midst of whatever denies us useful solitude. We must make up solitude where it does not exist.

Here you are again, coming to my aid, proving once again the reader, not the writer, has the keenest bead on the work. This time it is the voice of a dying man. We were visiting—death didn't come into it, you weren't expected to die. Not yet. Sometime, but not anytime soon. You're only a dying man in retrospect.

You liked to sit in the kitchen. That's where we were. You said you'd like a cup of coffee, and would I make it strong, please. With my back turned from you to your much-prized coffeemaker, you said, apropos of nothing, in a voice not personal, but decisive, quiet, calm: *You must always keep a part of your mind entirely to yourself.*

You weren't speaking generally, saying "one" should do this. You spoke directly to me, to the back of my head as if to the base of my existence. The voice of an oracle, a message like the one at the core of Western civilization—*Know thyself.* You repeated it, as if it had to be posted twice: *You must always keep a part of your mind entirely to yourself.*

Said mere days before your unexpected death. An odd, disconnected remark. Not part of the conversation we were having—we were talking about the dog who stood between us, and seemed to be listening. You were speaking of the absolute requirement of solitude not outside oneself as I had been "on retreat" in California. This was the solitude within the mind. This is integrity.

I was measuring the coffee into the coffeemaker. I didn't

turn around. I don't think you would have said it if I'd been facing you. You had to speak to the back of my head. It wasn't something to talk about across the yellow table. An oracle is like that, distant, implacable, penetrating. I added the water, listened to the thing bubbling.

I understood you were saying something essential, even though it was off-the-cuff. You were speaking—how strange I didn't realize it then—from a position almost on the other side of this surface we call life. Maybe I did sense that. Solitude itself was speaking to me.

I've come upon yet another example of solitude from Virginia Woolf, that writing virago who went from novels to essays to diary, on to letters, cycling back into fiction and nonfiction, an endless round of sentences for something like forty years. It sometimes seems, wearyingly, that she said just about everything a person could say about the life of the mind.

She was aware that she and her contemporaries at the dawn of what we call modernism were breaking with narrative tradition at some cost. She says about this new kind of writing that describes not the surface of action but the pulse of thought, "I have to create the whole thing afresh for myself each time. Probably all writers now are in the same boat. It is the penalty we pay for breaking with tradition, and the solitude makes the writing more exciting." Perhaps inevitably, she latches on to our word—*solitude*. It is an oddly personal word to describe the "penalty" of "breaking with tradition." She is describing a cultural separation, but one she experiences in bruising personal terms. And notice—"the solitude makes the writing more exciting."

Woolf was fretting—also preening—that this "new" narration of inner consciousness (her task, her "break with tradition") was something quite different, more coolly detached than "writing her life." To write her mind she was entering a solitude not romantic, but planetary. It was not autobiographical. She makes clear that this solitude is not about delving into the self. She even suggests a practical method to attain this solitude.

The first step, she says, is "gentle exercise in the air." This is not a metaphor. She means—go for a walk. Walk, let the world and the elements have at you. "Second, the reading of good literature. It is a mistake," she says, "to think that literature can be produced from the raw." That is, from the solo self, from "inside." Solitude is not a matter of consciously searching for originality of the unique "self." The opposite. The first step is physical exercise, the second is reading. Not writing, but reading. Getting into somebody else's head.

Curiously, the purpose she finds in solitude—or perhaps its lesson—is not to be alone with oneself. Solitude is not about discovering one's genius, one's misery or glory, one's *anything*. Not even one's life, Beckett's "my life, since we must call it so." Rather, she says in this diary entry, "one must become externalized; very, very concentrated . . . , not having to draw upon the scattered parts of one's character, living in the brain."

Get over yourself, in other words. This isn't about you. See yourself not as a source, not even as a subject, but as an

instrument. Montaigne's discovery in the *Essais*. This liberation from the ego is the purpose of solitude, to hone the blade
of the self to cut into reality, to bring a jagged piece of it back.
A shard. Don't expect to get the whole thing, the grail called
"form." You get maybe a shard. Put it in your pocket. Keep
walking in the open air.

It sounds lonely. But there is nothing to be afraid of here,
apparently. "The cure for loneliness," Marianne Moore advised,
"is solitude." What she is saying in her gnomic way is that loneliness is self-regarding, while solitude is world-regarding. Loneliness eats away at you. Solitude fills and fills you.

The testimony of contemplatives makes this clear, hermits
and cloistered nuns and monks who "leave the world," in order
to think of and pray about nothing else but the world and its
suffering. A failed monk is a monk trying to save himself. The
point of solitude for these professional solitaries is not to save
their souls, but to take on the reality of the world. That reality—
I'm only reporting here, see Buddha, see John of the Cross, see
Simone Weil—displays the fundamental facts of affliction and
beauty. Both. The poles of existence. The thorn and the rose. To
do this work, as the dying man told me, asking me to refill his
coffee—you liked it black in the little white mug—is that a part
of the mind must be kept separate. *Be still, and know that I am
God,* as the Psalmist says of the apprehension of reality.

Then there is Blaise Pascal with his lemon-sucking aphorism,
"All of humanity's problems stem from man's inability to sit
quietly in a room alone." Really? If we're going to think about

sitting quietly in a room alone, I'd rather think about Emily Dickinson, the white dresses, the upright house with the fence around it, the dense dark cakes given to neighbors, tiny poems in her spider hand on the bits of paper and the backs of envelopes, the snatches of reality she managed to cadge like crickets chirping in bamboo boxes. She took on the subject of solitude too, understanding it as cosmic, not personal, though to know and express that fact you have to become remote yourself, like a moon, cold and distant upon which reality is reflected. You have to keep part of your mind to yourself, separate, as you said, hands around your hot coffee mug. She figured out how to do that. This is her solitude poem:

> *HERE is a solitude of space,*
> *A solitude of sea,*
> *A solitude of death, but these*
> *Society shall be,*
> *Compared with that profounder site,*
> *That polar privacy,*
> *A Soul admitted to Itself:*
> *Finite Infinity.*

There's a woman who has sat in her room alone—and only allowed words in as her company. It's a much bigger condition than avoiding the troubles of the world. It is more like braving the troubles, shouldering them. Take a walk, in the open air, Pascal.

Thinking so long about solitude, I have arrived at poetry, of course, because poetry sets the campfire for solitude. My first love, and yours too—poems. The telltale shelves of the narrow paperbacks of contemporary poets that first day when you invited me in for a cup of coffee after showing me the garbage bins.

And I have arrived at mother and father—Emily and now Walt, that hugger-mugger working the room, hardly a poet we think of as a solitude man. But perhaps his thoughts about solitude are even truer to our condition as people who are not monks, but who long for love *and* for the privacy of mind. Here's Whitman's great solitude poem:

> I SAW in Louisiana a live-oak growing,
> All alone stood it, and the moss hung down from
>   the branches;
> Without any companion it grew there, uttering
>   joyous leaves of dark green,
> And its look, rude, unbending, lusty, made me
>   think of myself;
> But I wonder'd how it could utter joyous leaves,
>   standing alone there, without its friend, its lover
>   near—for I knew I could not;
> And I broke off a twig with a certain number of
>   leaves upon it, and twined around it a little
>   moss,
> And brought it away—and I have placed it in sight
>   in my room;
> It is not needed to remind me as of my own dear
>   friends,
> (For I believe lately I think of little else than of
>   them;)

> Yet it remains to me a curious token—it makes me
>   think of manly love;
> —For all that, and though the live-oak glistens
>   there in Louisiana, solitary, in a wide flat space,
> Uttering joyous leaves all its life, without a friend,
>   a lover, near,
> I know very well I could not.

There is a reading of this poem, current today, that sees it principally as a testament of sexual love, as surely it is. But it is also a poem of solitude and has about it some of the urgency I felt in that Rilke line all those years ago—*a love that consists in this, that two solitudes protect and touch and greet each other.* There is always this paradox in great passion—the desire to merge (or at least to be companioned) and the desire to be solitary, singular. The writer's dilemma. And the lover's.

Emily Dickinson's poem is more serene, more abstract than Whitman's. She speaks of the human condition as a contemplative. He of the human plight as a lover. "Solitude is fine," as Balzac said, "but you need someone to tell that solitude is fine." This is where being a writer comes in. Solitude is fine, but we need to tell the page, the screen, the reader, that it is. Dickinson may not have needed the reader. Whitman panted after him.

Like Beckett, we are beset with the inability to speak, with the inability to be silent, here in our solitude. But what, after all, is this solitude, what is it besides "being alone"? Kafka, always good for ratcheting up the misery quotient, said, "I need solitude for my writing; not like a hermit—that wouldn't be enough—but like a dead man." And wasn't it a man almost dead who said to me, holding the warmth of his coffee mug, speaking out of nowhere except from the need to say something essential before he would speak no more, *You need to keep part of your mind always to yourself.*

And what would that mean? If essential solitude is "keeping a part of your mind always to yourself," what does that look like? Feel like? What does it do to and for a writer? No, for anyone—we're in this together, reader, writer.

I find myself reaching back to the first contemporary poem I loved, a poem whose simplicity overwhelmed me. It's the first poem I taught to a group of students, when I was hardly older than they, in my hot little miniskirt and Frye boots at the University of Iowa in 1968. I have never stopped loving this poem, but I may only have begun to understand it. Maybe. Yet it's such a simple poem. I put it on our bedroom wall, and I have it "by heart," as we speak of memorization. James Wright's "Lying in a Hammock at William Duffy's Farm in Pine Island, Minnesota":

> *Over my head I see the bronze butterfly*
> *Asleep on the black trunk,*
> *Blowing like a leaf in green shadow.*
> *Down the ravine, behind the empty house,*
> *The cowbells follow one another*
> *Into the distances of the afternoon.*
> *To my right,*
> *In a field of sunlight between two pines,*
> *The droppings of last year's horses*

Blaze up like golden stones.
I lean back, as the evening darkens and comes
    on.
A chicken hawk floats over, looking for home.
I have wasted my life.

It was only many years after first reading it that I discovered Wright's final line—*I have wasted my life*—is a steal from or homage to Rilke's poem "Archaic Torso of Apollo." Rilke's poem is also built as a description—in his case of a fragment of a Greek statue. Wright knew Rilke's poem in the original German, and must have been dazzled by the startling final line that seems to have no logical or even associative connection with the poem's description. After taking three stanzas to describe the statue in all its detail, Rilke ends with the stern, unexplained finale: *You must change your life.*

When I discovered the Rilke poem, much later, it seemed to me that it had been influenced by Wright, not the other way round. It was Wright's poem that riveted me, describing a landscape I knew intimately, the landscape of my flyover state, a town barely an hour from my hometown. Just to see its name in a book of poetry thrilled me. Pine Island! Imagine, in a poem! And then, years later, you and I drove past Pine Island time and again on the freeway to the Mayo Clinic, that Lourdes we visited so faithfully, for a while a place of miracles.

Wright's poem bedeviled me for years. At first I thought the final line was a statement of defeat. It seemed brave, if sad. Some years later I felt smart and considerably more liter-ary when I decided no, *I have wasted my life* is a cry of triumph—I'm lying here in this hammock doing nothing and ha-ha on you out there working your lives away. I have the nerve to waste my life.

Much later still, very much later, with various betrayals and deaths and my own failures behind me and yet ever be-fore me, I realized that Wright *was* attesting to failure, but a very different failure than I had understood as a young poet enthralled with the idea of solitude and afraid of the life of love.

Here's how I've come to understand this apparently sim-ple poem: lying in the hammock the poet is alone, empty-minded. That is, he is living in solitude, the solitude of his mind. The world in its homely detail—sleeping butterfly, horse droppings—enters this solitude that is his conscious-ness. He realizes this has never happened to him before—he has never truly seen the world, its reality and detail. He is stunned to realize this. He has wasted his life precisely because he sees he has not wasted his life *enough*. Or really, at all until this moment. That was his mistake. He has not "failed" as I thought as a girl first reading the poem, imagining the defeat was that he was just describing a but-terfly, a wizened horse turd, a this, a that. I thought he was ashamed of his aimlessness, that he was valiantly articulat-ing his failure.

Nor did I understand the poem when I read it again in the ambition of my own first poems when I thought he was thumbing his arty nose at all the worker bees out there, that he was proudly claiming to be a free spirit who doesn't labor, and glories in lying around all day. He was a vainglorious lily of the field.

All wrong, I see now. He was acknowledging the waste of his life—that is, of his mind. But not for the reason I had thought. Rather, that final line—*I have wasted my life*—is suffused with wonder, the wonder of revelation that his experience in the hammock has given him. He is *finally* wasting his life. It's a conversion moment, I suppose. An exultant ah-ha!

He sees that this emptiness of self—that this alone—makes a life worth living, a life worth writing. He has been rinsed of ambition, of pride in himself, rinsed of shame over his failures, emptied of his grudges. He has even let go of time, of history—the sources of our regret, our sense that we have done it all wrong. Once reality has stabbed you in the heart like this, you are indeed free—or, when that sweet pain does leave you (Montaigne got that so right: it's about portraying *passing*), the realization remains, a sure memory. This realization, not your ego, is your true self. Alone, outside time, but paradoxically within the moment.

There he is, a poet suspended on planet earth in that most ephemeral piece of furniture, the hammock, swinging in the eternity of the moment, and he is empty of himself—at last. The whole world rushes in.

It's wildly ordinary—this moment of horse dung and cow-bells. And it's beautiful, and he can write it because, as the dying man advised—your last intelligence debriefed in the kitchen, holding the warm coffee mug I had handed you—his mind is separate. It rests in the solitude that opens, finally, fully, to the world.

Is that what you were saying, darling, my face turned away, your voice coming to me from the other side you were approaching?

The dog has curled up on the dark navy back deck cushion, her place. And the coffee theme advances, this time my hand holding one of the blue willow cups we bought in that Prairie du Chien secondhand store, a whole set for the boat because you had read that it was the pattern used on riverboats in the nineteenth century.

I still come down here, sit, read, stare out at the river as the barges go by this scruffy city marina tucked under the High Bridge. We never thought of mooring the boat out of the city, on the prettier (people say) St. Croix. We wanted a working river, wanted to be at the Mississippi headwaters, the beginning of the great waterway to the sea. The barges drift along in their stately way, nudged forth by chubby workboats called tows or tugs, though in fact they *push* the barges from behind, no tugging or towing involved. We remarked on that, our usual preoccupation with words, words. Must look that up, you said—why they're towboats, not pushboats. Never got around to that.

It's a ragged 1940 Chris-Craft cabin cruiser, a woody you bought while we were "courting" (that antique term you used). It was as if you'd tossed an old Steinway in the water. You'd always wanted a boat, a Kansas boy long in love with water— your Elsewhere. But you got the Chris-Craft, you told me later, to romance me—*After a whirlwind courtship of eight years,* you liked to say, *we got married.* But really, you had me at the garbage bins the day I moved into the apartment above yours.

The boat has a deco look, as if Bogart might step out of the main saloon with a shaker of martinis. A boat just big enough (thirty-three feet) for us to pretend it was a cottage— back deck like a little porch where I sit looking out, the mahogany saloon outfitted with chairs, table, the chrome-fitted steering wheel, windows that roll down like car windows, then a few steps down to the tiny galley (starboard side) and, tinier still, the head (port side). Forward, the jewel box of the V-berth, our nest, a round hatch at the top of the silky white-painted chamber, fitted with a screen, nights when we had to scramble to pull down the hatch when it rained. That we loved, rain tapping on the little wooden craft, our legs twined under the cloud of the marine blue duvet, thunder, lightning, curled up together in the chamber of wood, as if within a perfectly tuned musical instrument.

"There is nothing—absolutely nothing—half so much worth doing," Rat informs Mole in *The Wind in the Willows,* "as simply messing about in boats." He speaks with the domestic satisfaction of the householder, not the adventure-voice of the seafarer. Cabin cruisers and houseboats play a watery riff on the art of housekeeping. Mornings we climbed onto the forward deck with a can of Brasso to polish the chrome fittings, the boat bobbing like a well-rocked cradle in the marina slip. Not to mention your fiddling belowdeck with the engine, the generator, the bilge pumps. This marine housecleaning is not to be confused with dusting the dining room chairs or vacuuming the rug at home. It's messing about in boats. It's domestic romance.

Whole seasons can go by—and did—in a round of such fantasy housekeeping, interrupted by picnic rides out of the marina up to the confluence of the Mississippi and the Minnesota rivers, one dark steel, the other golden brown, past Fort Snelling, high on the bluff, the fact of the sprawling metropolitan area erased, as we drifted by stands of oak, past a heron rookery, a tangle of old cottonwood roots exposed in the mud.

The boat returned contentedly to the slip like a nag glad to regain her stall. Not to mention—though I want to mention all of it, all those years—the sheer dreamy frittering of time, sitting on the back deck reading to the end of *Villette,* one of those fat novels I always meant to finish, getting up to make coffee in the marine-spruce galley, a rare place-for-everything-everything-in-its-place place. At twilight the plush emerald-headed mallards moved from boat to boat along the little community marina where some of the boats were year-round homes for live-aboards, and we stood on the back deck tossing bits of bread into the water.

The long afternoons swooned into night, and it was time to switch on the radio, catch the Twins losing again as the dark water sent up gleaming reflections from the city lights. A soft bobbing like a riverine heartbeat whenever a barge passed by, shedding faint waves toward shore. "That's the charm of it," Rat explains. "You're always busy, and you never do anything in particular."

We talked for years about taking a big trip downriver. We had the river, we had the boat, frail old craft that she was. We seemed only to lack the gumption. Where to go? New Orleans? Too ambitious. St. Louis? Still too far, and word in the marina was that the best scenery on the river was our own—the Upper Mississippi above Dubuque.

We settled finally on Prairie du Chien, Wisconsin, as our destination, about two hundred miles south of St. Paul, an easy day trip by car. But with our sedate Hercules Flathead 6 engine (rebuilt) conducting herself like a dowager royal, we only made ten miles an hour, tops, going with the current, considerably less on the upriver return. Two weeks, down and back up. Doable.

Prairie du Chien had another appeal. There, at the mouth of the Wisconsin River, the veteran *voyageur* Louis Jolliet, along with Père Jacques Marquette, a Jesuit trained as a cartographer and fluent in several Indian languages, canoed with their Indian guides down the Fox and Wisconsin rivers from their raw station of St. Ignace, and arrived finally on June 17, 1673, at their long-imagined destination: the Mississippi. Marquette's diary notation is the first European record of an encounter with the river. We were traveling not simply to a place, but to a point in history.

We studied the guidebooks and river charts—"Think we

can make Red Wing in a day?" we wondered, speaking with real worry about a town barely an hour away by car. We decided to take two days, better not chance it. By the time we departed in mid-July, when we spoke of going to Prairie du Chien, we sounded as if we were embarking for Cathay.

The charts were littered with the names of landings and sloughs without road access or populations, places long forgotten or never settled, abandoned except by the agate type of the river charts: Winters Landing, Coon Middle Daymark, Ruby Ferry Light, Bad Ax Island, Betsy Slough and Millstone Landing, Canton Chute, Winfield Access, Shady Creek, and my favorite, Point No Point.

Reading these names gave presence to anonymous and unmarked islands, the sandy or forested riverbanks we passed. The absence of habitation attached to a place name made the very real landscape somehow an imaginative construct. Point No Point, indeed. The river pooled and spread, opening at sudden turns into inlets and back channels where we could not go. Only shallow-draft boats, canoes, and johnboats could explore those mysterious byways. We held to the channel, nine feet deep, that the Corps of Engineers had dredged for the tows, a public works project dating from the Depression, looking off to the named places, hidden and somehow imaginary, existing only in the words given them on the charts.

The tidy canal-like channel of the river we knew in downtown St. Paul gave way to an island-studded relay of industrial parks and generous suburban lots, the riversides heavy with parked barges, and finally a sewage plant up against a heron rookery, one of the major bird sanctuaries on the great Mississippi flyway. White egrets, refined as Egyptian ibis, streaked over the water, landing their minimal forms on the gray bleached driftwood lying in the shallows, composed together like a collection of Brancusi sculptures.

We followed the channel, obeying the markers, as the river opened up, threading our course around uninhabited islands, keeping the illusion we were moving on a straight and narrow waterway. But even as we kept thinking of the river as a line running down the middle of the country, it revealed itself as a massive conspiracy of waterways, a feuding, feeding clan of intermarried streams and related watercourses perfectly capable of spilling over almost a third of the American landmass at its heart—as it had in the historic floods of 1993, when we were still treating the boat as a cabin, sitting snug in our marina slip. Left to its own devices (if ever that was—even the Ojibwe made dams and rudimentary fordings), the Upper Midwest is a vast wetland. At our center we are not "the heartland," but islands adrift in a waterland, individualism not simply an American idea, but a fact of our geography.

Our trip was punctuated by brief dramas of "locking through" the nine locks between St. Paul and Prairie du Chien. You were pretty convincing at the wheel, your face still and steady, pulling the grand piano we had unwisely set afloat right up to the side of the wet mossy cement lock wall. I lurched around madly grabbing for the line the lockkeeper slung down.

But these were frantic interludes in the long, dreamy progress through a landscape that became increasingly improbable, beautiful—sublime in a way the Midwest is not *supposed* to be. Gone the farmlands and prairies, gone the featureless flyover I had fretted against all my girlhood and beyond. The modesty and long horizons of the Midwest's usual rural charms (never charming to me looking for the great world, my real estate searches for châteaus and seaside cottages in Brittany)—all this usual expectation and assumption about the landscape gave way, between Red Wing and La Crosse, to high romantic vistas, arrays of sheer-face palisades and bluffs that effectively erased the dairy farms, the corn and bean fields that lay beyond them. The whole length of the trip we saw only one silo, set high in the distance like a campanile. *Move over, castles on the Rhine,* you said as we passed Trempeleau on the Wisconsin side.

We were not in the pioneer farmscape of the nineteenth century, but further back to the terrain of the French and Indian hunters and traders, the explorers of the seventeenth century, almost back to Montaigne's *homme simple et grossier,* his simple crude fellow who could report to him on the creatures of the New World, the men living naked and free.

Nowhere does the Midwest feel as ancient. Or as unmarked, even with the intrusion of the locks and dams. To experience this time travel, the dislocation of history, we had to be on the river. We had taken the same trip many times by car, down the Minnesota side, up the Wisconsin side. But never these views, the theatrical palisades obscuring with a tease, and then revealing a whole panorama of interlocked channels and inlets, even grander bluffs plunging into the river as the boat rounded an island curve. Somewhere there were bean fields, somewhere apple orchards, dairy farms and all that cheese, but here, low down in the channel, the passage was caught in the older drift of history and the memory of bark canoes.

The camaraderie of real travel, of those meeting off the beaten trail and needing the kindness of strangers, was ours too. From Prescott, our first stop, all the way to Prairie du Chien, the marinas where we rented a slip each night proved to be worlds of their own, transient communities with the easy friendliness of campgrounds. At Prescott the marina owner gave us a bag of charcoal so we could use the grill in the town park pitched above the river. I stood on the grassy rise, glass of wine in hand, turning the chicken, gazing out at the confluence where the deep blue ribbon of the St. Croix cuts into the golden brown of the Mississippi. Next to the grill a bronze plaque marked the place: "In 1680 Explorers Hennepin and DuLhut passed this point."

The bag of charcoal was not the only kindness offered by strangers. At every marina, people jumped off their boats to help us land and cast off, emerging from their houseboats, then drifting courteously away again. In La Crosse, we walked from our slip at Pettibone Marina along the highway in the dark until we arrived at a convenience store/office of a campground that had a laundromat. While we were paying for a carton of milk, we mentioned to the owner of the place, a tired-looking man who must have put in a long day, that we were docked at Pettibone and had walked over. Too bad we hadn't known about the laundromat, I said, hard to find places to do laundry on the river.

"Here," he said, and handed over his car keys. "Drive over to Pettibone and bring your laundry over to wash." He wouldn't take our driver's licenses, didn't even glance at them as we tried to push them on him as collateral. We climbed into his Chrysler, the radio tuned to the C&W station, and headed back to the marina.

I realized I was clutching the sides of the car seat on the highway as you drove. Cars, everything, seemed to be going so *fast*. It felt mad. I was glad—you said you were too—relieved really, to return the Chrysler to the trusting man, do the laundry, walk back to the boat with our clean clothes folded and stowed in our backpacks. We were glad to be walking, restored to the sanity of river time, river speed.

The towns on the Wisconsin side, from Maiden Rock and Stockholm past Pepin and Alma, were charming hamlets, their rough brick buildings cast at river's edge against the swelling bluffs and magnificent heights that rose behind them. We got halfway across Lake Pepin, the big bulge in the river—too far to turn back to Red Wing, still distant from Wabasha at the lower tip—when the Coast Guard station came on the marine radio with a tornado warning. The sky, which had been pastel, looked suddenly bruised and angry. There was nothing to do but follow the channel, fingers crossed. Your face a mask of calm. But I could read you, alarm in your hazel eyes.

Luck was with us. The tornado dematerialized. We spent the night in a state of grateful reprieve, rocking under the tin-covered slip at the Wabasha Marina, the rain making pinging sounds on the corrugated roof as the barn swallows flew in and out. We lay in the cutty cabin, looking out the round hatch—at nothing, I thought—when a great blue heron sailed by, its flight caught in the frame of the hatch as if in the lens of a camera. An instant. Boats, tethered to the creaking wooden slips, rubbed against their bumpers, sighing and groaning like well-fed beasts.

Wabasha was our favorite marina. I was swapping out châteaus for boat slips—*Let's bring the boat down here next year for the whole summer!* Your laconic reply from the helm: *We could.*

But Fountain City and Trempealeau, farther south, were our favorite towns, sweet old villages, their grandeur well behind them, but their locations a lasting reward, nestled below palisades where the river spread like a great creased cloak thrown before them in permanent homage.

"Wouldn't it be great," I said as we headed toward the municipal dock (there was no marina), "if Fountain City had a soda fountain?"

For once, wishing made it so. At the Corner Store, an old brick-face pharmacy turned into an antique store/soda fountain/laundromat, run as a hobby by a retired nurse named Fran, we ordered our sodas, chocolate (you) and caramel (me). A steady stream of children stopped by, checked their penny piles, stacks of their change Fran banked for them on the ledge above her old-style cash register, credit accounts she kept for each child.

As we headed into the back-channel marina on St. Feriole Island, having finally achieved Prairie du Chien, we could no longer ignore a distinct gas smell. The fume sensor was still on green, barely, but we docked knowing we had a problem.

The St. Feriole marina was a funky place, run by an extended family, everyone apparently related or married to someone else. Like so much of the life along the river this far north, it felt oddly southern, as if on a bayou backwater and not in Wisconsin dairyland. Here we found the mechanic of our marine dreams, a man who never gave us his name, who conducted himself like a great, aloof surgeon.

He saw instantly what was wrong. With the laconic manner that is the signal of authority in a mechanic, he set about repairing the engine. He did allow himself to remark on the numerous *imbeciles* with whom he had to consort: government gas pump inspectors, irresponsible boaters who had no business on the river, and especially the misguided mechanics across the river in McGregor who didn't know how to work on engines like ours, men who contented themselves with the contemptible craft of servicing outboards. What kind of life was that? he wanted to know.

Somewhere, clearly, in the midst of his essentially benign contempt, there was a niche for us, city folk with an old boat we hardly understood. He did have respect for the boat itself. Unlike the admirers who complimented us along the way, he said nothing about the wood, the chrome, the fine plumb bow. He simply noted that if every engine were made as simply as this Hercules Flathead 6, life in general would present fewer problems.

We cast off the next morning, for the first time headed

north. Toward home. Upriver on the Wisconsin side, the bluffs rose and fell in shades of green, strands of granite and sandstone showing in horizontal strips.

On the Iowa side, the shore mounted steeply in a dense canopy of trees. No houses, no railroad to be seen, no highway. Some driftwood and boulders, no real beach, just the forest rising abruptly from the river in great florets like giant broccoli.

It was another of the river's uncanny seventeenth-century moments, the untouched waterway presenting itself with nonchalant majesty, sky and water contriving to convey an early morning muddle of pastel light and mist.

We emerged from the backwater, turned the old woody into the magnificent channel, seeing it freshly, even as Père Marquette had when he noted that first European sighting with such emotion, writing in his diary the summer of 1673. Though we were headed home, and not into the unknown as he was, we entered the river as he said he and Jolliet and their Indian leaders had—*with a joy I cannot express.*

The dog has stretched, and I think she wants to get off the boat. But no, she rearranges herself, curls more tightly into herself on the navy cushion. She's the one deciding things now. She has me well trained. We'll stay awhile longer, softly bobbing in the slip. Dusk, and the low-riding hulk of a three-barge chain goes silently past, its high white tow behind like a bodyguard.

I don't use the boat for trips now. That big trip to deepest

Prairie du Chien turned out to be the adventure of a lifetime. After all my gallivanting, my lust for Elsewhere. It was my comeuppance, barely two hundred miles from St. Paul, and the greatest travel experience of my life, the time when—almost—I touched history, was *in* it. You the pilot, I holding the charts as if I could read them.

I haven't sold the old boat, not yet. It's turned back now to its earlier stay-at-home self, a craft that is a cabin. That's all right, one trip like that is enough for a lifetime. It's everything. To go or to stay? In the boat, on the river, we could do both at the same time. Years of mending the paradox of choice, not just the life of being—that other elusive life. The life that *portrays passing*.

And didn't we love, those weeks of the big trip to Prairie du Chien, just the same as here in our home slip, sitting on the back deck, idling away the night, taking our leisure in the morning? Letting time have its way with us, living Montaigne's great idea:

We say; "I have done nothing today." What, have you not lived? That is not only the fundamental but the most illustrious of your occupations . . .

The point the man in his old stone tower is making, still speaking to the woman alone in her old wooden boat, is that this life is not about accomplishment. Maybe it isn't even about love, darling.

We are here, he says, *to compose our character.* This, alone, he insists, *is our duty, not to compose books, and to win, not battles and provinces, but order and tranquility in our conduct. Our great and glorious masterpiece is to live appropriately.* To do this you must be idle. He says this in his *Essai* titled—what else?—"On Idleness."

We loved the sound of the dove, you and I, the coo of longing that often woke us mornings on the river, though we never succeeded in luring one to the little courtyard garden by the alley at home. You researched dove nests, made one in the basement, mounted it in the poet's tree—the laurel, the very sapling the city was planting the day I moved into the apartment above yours. The day you walked me to the garbage bins. And then we had a cup of coffee, and I saw your shelf of contemporary poetry books. You mounted the dove nest in the laurel tree and waited. Nobody came.

You wrote an impassioned letter to the Minnesota legislature protesting the legalization of a state dove hunting season. Left it on my desk: *Drst: Edit this for me, will you? See if I've made my point.*

We wondered if the word was *mourning dove*—or was it *morning dove*? We meant to look it up—we were always looking things up. But we hadn't gotten around to that. An argument could be made for either word—the sadness of the low cooing, the welcoming of the day when we most often heard that sweet aching sound. Mourning, morning.

Which is it, darling? Can't remember or never knew. But I have the time now, don't I? Another thing I really must look up.

Acknowledgments

For initial confirmation and substantial support for time and travel, abiding thanks to the University of Minnesota Regents Professor research fund, to the Corporation of Yaddo and the Bogliasco Foundation for welcome residencies, and for generous support from The Project on Lived Theology at the University of Virginia where some of the ideas here first hatched.

Montaigne had his cold tower, but I have had generous friends offering warm perches in dream landscapes, providing companionship as well as solitude, a rare and paradoxical gift. With loving gratitude to Stacey Mills Heins and Samuel D. Heins, Rosemarie Johnstone and Ben Weinstein, to Rosanne Haggerty and Lloyd Sederer, to Maria Krausová and Dagmar Hlusicková, and to Annette Kobak on the road and in London. And to the late Phebe Hanson.

A book finds its readers because those essential first readers—agent and editor—believe there is a book in its pages. To Marly Rusoff, most valiant agent, and Paul Slovak, patient and acute editor, a deep bow.

Finally, to Terrence Williams, dearest reader, a heavy debt of gratitude I gladly bear with love, still and ever.